The King, the Maiden, and the Prize

Karyl Simmons

Published by BookLocker.com, Inc., Bradenton, Florida.

Printed in the United States of America.

BookLocker.com, Inc.
2014

First Edition

Dedication

This, my first book, is dedicated to my husband, Billy, who has demonstrated a true shepherd's heart to me. Together we have walked with our Beloved through 50 plus years of marriage in this wilderness of life and he has always been a source of strength, encouragement, and inspiration to me. I can truly say that he is a man after God's heart.

TABLE OF CONTENTS

PREFACE

In studying this marvelous book of the Bible, "The Song of Solomon," I have come to realize that there are numerous variations of interpretation of this song and its applications to our lives. It is valuable in a study on marriage or in a study of Jesus and His church.

In the Holman Illustrated Bible Dictionary I found these words about the Song of Solomon: "The whole world is not worth the day on which the Song of Songs was given to Israel; all the writings are holy, but the Song of Songs is the Holy of Holies."[1] This is a quote from Rabbi Akiva, one of the scholars who helped to canonize the Bible.

I have also discovered many of the major doctrines of the Bible within the content of this book. In fact, it could be called "The Gospel According to the Song of Solomon."

There are many characters in the song and all of them – except for Solomon, the Holy Spirit, and Satan and his forces – represent people in various relational positions to the King. A Christian may identify with many of the characters in the song and hopefully so. Christianity is not a religion, it is a relationship.

As I seek to relate to the church the truths that I feel the Holy Spirit has taught me from the song, it causes me to reflect much on the admonition in I Timothy 2:15 that instructs us to be diligent to show ourselves approved to God – workmen who do not need to be ashamed – workmen who are able to handle accurately the Word of Truth. I pray continually, asking the Holy Spirit to guide me into all truth as I handle the Word, for I know it is able to divide soul from spirit, bone from marrow and it will judge my thoughts and the intentions of my heart.

I would like to express my heartfelt thanks to those who have come along side me to help me in my endeavor to follow the instruction of the Lord; to make this vital message from the "Song of Solomon" available to His church. Special thanks go to Tommy and Kay Smart, to Mike Shurley, and to Sandy Angle.

It is my prayer that the Holy Spirit will speak to you, Christian, from the pages of this book, "The King, the Maiden, and the Prize." I pray that it will be instrumental in preparing you for our Lord's soon return and that it will inspire you to press on to do those things that will enable you to lay hold of the Prize and your destiny in the Kingdom of Heaven.

---

[1] Holman Illustrated Bible Dictionary

INTRODUCTION

In the past few years, and especially in the last few months, the Holy Spirit has been speaking to me with a real sense of urgency that time is a precious commodity and it is not to be misused. As I hear men and women of God express the Father's heart to His people, many of them seem to be giving the same message. It is the message that I have sensed coming from the throne room as well and that is --- prepare --- prepare --- prepare the way of the Lord and **prepare yourselves for His coming**.

There are priceless treasures to be found in the Word of God that will prepare us for the days ahead and I want to give you some tools with which to dig from the Song of Solomon that will help you to find some of these treasures.

If you, Christian, are feeling the call of the Bridegroom wooing you into a deeper, more intimate relationship with Him; if you long to know Him better and to know more of His life changing truths; if you have sensed the Holy Spirit at work in you, preparing you to embrace your destiny and you have determined to become all that God intended you to be, the Lord will use the song mightily in your life as you hunt for the treasures that are buried there. The Bible speaks of the Prize and it would greatly benefit you, Christian, to seek after and lay hold of it. It is referred to in Matthew 13:44 as the pearl of great price - a real treasure to be found in the Kingdom of Heaven and we will discover what that prize is, that pearl, the great treasure in the song and what we must do in order to lay hold of it.

But be prepared, Christian, to encounter the adversary and his schemes to use whatever means he can to distract and discourage you from your determination to know and move towards your destiny as you seek to gain the prize in God's Kingdom. You need to be aware of his tactics for he does not want you to have it!

This lovely, passionate book tells of a journey that transforms a lowly, ordinary Shulamite shepherdess into "The only one – the perfect one" who ravishes the King's heart and it tells how she becomes His glorious bride. This song is rich in beautiful symbolism and speaks allegorically of Jesus, the Bridegroom King and His bride, the bride of Christ. It is the most remarkable love story ever told.

An allegory is a literary, dramatic, or pictorial device in which each character, object and event symbolically illustrates a moral or religious principle.[2] You will also see in this song what is referred to as a paradox, a statement that seems to conflict with common sense or to contradict itself but that may nevertheless be true.[3]

There are key words in each verse of this song that are rich with symbolic meaning and that give the reader a depth of insight to understand all that is being said in that verse. The writer of the song takes natural things and gives them spiritual meanings. We see this often throughout the scriptures. We must look to the Bible to see how these words are used in scripture and to the Greek and Hebrew meanings to determine the spiritual connotation of these key words. Much of that research had already been done by authors like Bob and Rose Wiener in their study book, "Bible Studies for the Preparation of the Bride,' and by Mike Bickle in his book, "Song of Songs."

It fascinates me to read the various translations of the song. None of them are exactly the same, and none of the various books that I've read on this subject interpret the song in the same way. The Song of Solomon is often referred to as a mysterious book. In Ephesians we find these words referring to Christ and the church within the context of marriage:

---

[2] Webster's II Dictionary
[3] Webster's II Dictionary

1

This is a great mystery, but I speak concerning Christ and the church. (Eph. 5:32, NKJV)

I would encourage you, Christian, to ask the Holy Spirit to reveal to you those truths from the song that would draw you closer to our Beloved Bridegroom King and that would inspire you to greater service to him.

Mike Bickle, pastor and author, says this in his study of the song, "There is going to be a revival of interest in the Song of Solomon in the final generation. The Holy Spirit will cause the song to become prominent again and will raise up men and women, young and old, that will proclaim it, sing it, write about it and intercede it back to God until a <u>revival of holy passion</u> breaks out worldwide. Already we are enjoying new songs of intimacy with bridal themes that extol the beauty of Jesus as seen in the "Song of Songs."[4]

Beloved, if this be so, then the Holy Spirit will use this song mightily in these last days before Jesus' return to prepare the bride. I believe the Holy Spirit is speaking to us today through the Song of Solomon!

We are going to find the key words in each verse and expound upon them and their meanings. Then, using the symbolic meanings, I will attempt to relate the message which I feel the Holy Spirit is conveying, in laymen's terms of today that we are all able to understand.

This book may be used individually or in a group setting with a moderator or teacher and may be used with or without visual aids. There are several illustrations that have been provided for your edification. The following methods are employed to aid you in comprehending the material in this text:

The verses are in bold letters.

The symbol "●" indicates key words.

Italics indicate how the key words are interpreted.

Scripture references are used in accordance with the instructions provided in the New King James Version of the Bible.

May the Lord bless you mightily as you study this text and may you gain understanding of how the Song of Solomon applies to modern life.

- Karyl Simmons

---

[4] Song of Songs by Mike Bickle

CHAPTER ONE

THE KISS

VERSE 1

The song of songs which is Solomon's.

There are two main characters in the song and Solomon is one of them. His name means peace and in this allegory, Solomon represents the Bridegroom, Jesus.

- *The song is symbolic of one's spiritual walk or journey through life.*

This book is like a musical drama that tells a story using many characters. You will most likely find yourself somewhere in this song and, hopefully, you will be encouraged to press on to the goal of the Prize of the upward call of God in Christ Jesus. We will be discussing the Prize further in the next verse.

There are many songs mentioned and recorded in the Word:

> **Rev. 5:9 – The song of the redeemed.**
> **Rev. 14:3 – The song that only the 144,000 Jews can sing.**
> **Rev. 15:3-4 The song of Moses and the Lamb**
> **Zeph. 3:12 "Did you know that there are songs which God sings to you and me?" (NKJV)**

The Psalms of David are full of songs that he wrote. King David was the man who the word says was "a man after God's own heart." There are many anointed songs that Christians enjoy today written by gifted song writers who love the Lord and His Word. But this song, a song that Solomon (a man whose wisdom according to I Kings 4:30, "…excelled that of all other men" (NKJV)) wrote, is the "Song of all Songs!"

VERSE 2

THE SHULAMITE (speaking to all):

"Let Him kiss me with the kisses of His mouth,

(She then turns to Solomon and says)

For your love is better than wine."

The Shulamite is the other main character in this drama and she is speaking to the characters that are mentioned in this scene. The scene takes place outside the King's chambers and those present are the Shulamite, the King, and the daughters of Jerusalem. Shulamite means daughter of peace. We will see this maiden, who is not at peace at this point in the song, become an instrument of peace in chapter six and she will become as one who finds peace at the close of the song. She represents one who is born again and who is an integral part of the church of the living God. Allegorically, she represents the bride of Christ.

- ***The kisses are to embrace discipline and receive instruction.***

It is God's invitation to the "casual" Christian to seek a more intimate relationship with Jesus, to absorb His Word, and to allow it to train one in Godliness.

> **Ps. 2:12 "Kiss the Son lest He be angry and you perish in the way when his wrath is kindled but a little." (NKJV)**

- ***His mouth is symbolic of His speech.***

> **Matt. 4:4 But He answered and said, "It is written, man shall not live by bread alone but by every word that proceeds from the mouth of God." (NKJV)**

These divine kisses of instruction and discipline that come from God's mouth are communicated to us today in many ways. They come primarily through personal meditation on the Word, but they can also come through sermons, songs, and testimonies of others, through prophetic revelation of the Holy Spirit in a vision or a dream, and through Bible based counseling, etc. These kisses will groom us to take our place in God's kingdom where we are citizens.

We cannot afford as Christians to be ignorant, indifferent, or lazy about our destiny in God's kingdom, and neither is the maiden of this song as we see her make this request for the King's kisses. It is clear to me that she is after something and she must have His kisses in order to get it. I believe that she is after "...the goal of the prize of the upward call of God in Christ Jesus."

I also believe, after studying the song, that the prize is the **matchless life transforming love of the Bridegroom King for His bride!** We will see, as we study the song further, that seeking after this bridal love will eventually create in the maiden a capacity to return this most excellent love to the King as she is changed from glory to glory.

> **II Cor. 3:18 "But we all, with unveiled face, beholding as in a mirror the glory of the Lord, are being transformed into the same image from glory to glory just as by the Spirit of the Lord." (NKJV)**

Now we all know that God loves us even while we were yet sinners and lost in the world, but this love is that and more. It is the love of the Bridegroom for his bride, the ultimate prize. The Apostle, Paul, speaks of this prize:

> **Phil. 3:14 "I press toward the goal for the prize of the upward call of God in Christ Jesus." (NKJV)**

Paul also speaks of the prize in Corinthians when he talks about those who run in the race. He tells us to run to win the prize:

> **I Cor. 9:24 "Do you not know that those who run in a race all run, but one receives the prize? Run in such a way that you may obtain it." (NKJV)**

In verse four of this chapter, we will see the maiden of the song promising to run with her Beloved in this kingdom race as she pursues the prize. At the close of the song we will see her find her place in God's Kingdom at the side of her Bridegroom King as His bride-queen. Studying her journey will give you and me the inspiration to follow her example in her pursuit of the prize.

We are told in Matthew 11:12 that the Kingdom of God suffers violence and that the violent take it by force! The Greek meaning of the word, violence, is to "force, to crowd one's self into, to be seized, to press." We are to press forward in this race with violence in our effort to seize the prize.

It is this prize that we all seek in our life's journey. In striving to gain it, we are transformed and we become like Jesus, as we will discover in this "Song of Songs." In reaching for the prize, we move toward our destiny in God's kingdom; to sit at Jesus' side in order to rule and reign with Him as His glorious bride-queen. We will gain the prize if we press toward the goal, never giving up, and if we endure the fullness of testing that perfects us for "that day."

> **Heb. 12: 1-2 "Therefore we also, since we are surrounded by so great a cloud of witnesses, let us lay aside every weight and the sin which so easily ensnares us, and let us run with endurance the race that is set before us, looking unto Jesus, the author and finisher of our faith, who for the joy that was set before Him endured the cross, despising the shame, and has sat down at the right hand of God." (NKJV)**

We will see the maiden in this song experience the cold north wind of adversity. She experiences the hills and mountains of challenges and obstacles. She experiences the testing that would separate her from her Beloved if she allows it. The Holy Spirit will use these "tests" to refine her and prepare her to take her place in God's Kingdom as the glorious bride at the side of her King. We will see her finally embrace her destiny in the Kingdom of God, but only after she has endured the fullness of testing.

The maiden says to Solomon:

"Your love is better than wine."

- *Wine is symbolic of the joy of the Holy Spirit at work in one's life*

The maiden says that His love is better than wine because His bridal love for His bride-queen and the bride-queen's passionate love for the King is the Prize, and it is the end result of the joyful work of the Holy Spirit in her life.

Eccl. 7:18a "The end result is better than the beginning..."

In ancient Jewish tradition (which both Solomon and Jesus observed), when a man approached a young maiden and her family with a contract of marriage, there were a number of things that took place. One was that a cup of wine was shared between the prospective groom and the bride's family after they had agreed upon the terms of the marriage contract. If the bride accepted the cup and drank the wine as well, then she also was agreeing to the contract and, by drinking the cup of wine, she was saying, "Yes, I will prepare myself to become your bride!" This sealed the contract.

Christian, this is a picture of what happens today when we accept Jesus and drink in the Holy Spirit which allows His sanctifying work to begin to change our lives. The Holy Spirit is the third person of the Trinity. When Jesus was preparing to leave this world and go to the Father, he told us that He would send the Holy Spirit to come and remain with us forever.

> **John 16:7 "Nevertheless I tell you the truth. It is to your advantage that I go away for if I do not go away, the Helper will not come to you, but if I depart, I will send Him to you." (NKJV)**

> **John 16:13 "However, when He, the Spirit of truth, has come, He will guide you in all truth; ..."**

We receive the Holy Spirit when we invite Jesus into our lives.

> **John 20:22 "He breathed on them, and said to them, "Receive the Holy Spirit, ..."**

And then, God promises that Jesus will baptize us with the Holy Spirit and with fire that will transform us. Jesus spoke these words to his disciples:

> **Acts 1:4-5 "On one occasion, while He was eating with them, He gave them this command, "Do not leave Jerusalem, but wait for the gift My Father promised, which you have heard Me speak about. For John baptized with water, but in a few days you will be baptized with the Holy Spirit."" (NIV)**

John the Baptist spoke these words about Jesus, concerning this matter in the Gospel of Matthew:

> **Matt. 3:11 "I indeed baptize you with water unto repentance but He who is coming after me is mightier than I whose sandals I am not worthy to carry. He will baptize you with the Holy Spirit and fire." (NKJV)**

> **John 7:37-38 "On this last day, that great day of the feast, Jesus stood and cried out, saying, "If anyone thirsts, let him come to Me and drink. He who believes in Me, as the scripture has said, out of His heart will flow rivers of living water."" (NKJV)**

Jesus was speaking here of the Holy Spirit. He did not leave us orphans...He left the Holy Spirit to abide with us and in us.

> **John 14:16-18 "And I will ask of the Father, and He will give you another Counselor to be with you forever—the spirit of truth. The world cannot accept Him, because it neither sees Him nor knows Him. But you know Him, for He lives with you and will be in you. I will not leave you as orphans; I will come to you." (NIV)**

I believe that our soul (heart and mind) is then sealed to Jesus by the Holy Spirit when we receive Him. What is it to be "sealed" by God with the Holy Spirit? Webster gives a long list of meanings for this word, seal, but there are two that seem to apply in this instance:

1. Something that confirms, ratifies, or makes secure: Guarantee, assurance.

2. To fasten with or as if with a seal to prevent tampering.

When we receive the Holy Spirit to abide in us, He is our guarantee that we belong to Jesus and no one else has the authority to tamper with us.

> **II Cor. 1:21-22 "Now He who establishes us with you in Christ and has anointed us is God, who also has sealed us and given us the Spirit in our hearts as a guarantee. (NKJV)**

> **Eph. 1:12 "...in whom also having believed, you were sealed with the Holy Spirit of promise." (NKJV)**

> **Eph. 4:30 "And do not grieve the Holy Spirit of God, by whom you were sealed for the day of redemption." (NKJV)**

Then when Jesus baptizes us in the Holy Spirit and with fire, the refining process begins in us and transforms us into His glorious, spotless bride.

Today in communion, when we take the cup of wine, we are reminded of our covenant with the King and of our part in that covenant. We are saying to our Bridegroom, Jesus, "Yes, I have accepted your contract of marriage and I will allow the Holy Spirit to prepare me for our wedding day!"

I believe the Shulamite had already accepted the cup of wine at this point in the drama, and now, she is about to experience the joy of the Holy Spirit at work in her life that will prepare her to embrace her destiny and take her place in the Kingdom as the King's bride-queen.

> **Eph. 5:18-19 "And do not be drunk with wine, in which is dissipation, but be filled with the Spirit, speaking to one another in Psalms and hymns and spiritual songs, singing and making melody in your heart to the Lord." (NKJV)**

This is a picture of the joy of the Holy Spirit at work in us.

- *Wine is also symbolic of the blood of Jesus.*

In the ancient Jewish tradition of marriage there was a bride price that had to be agreed upon before the contract was sealed. It was a costly price that the bridegroom was required to pay for the bride. The bride price that Jesus paid for you and me was His shed blood on the cross of Calvary. Every time you drink the wine in communion which represents his blood, the blood of the new covenant, you are remembering the costly bride price that Jesus paid for you. You and I are very precious to Him.

In Summary

The wine speaks of our wonderful salvation; it speaks of the fire of the Holy Spirit that works in out lives to cleanse and refine us so that we can move on to our destiny in God's Kingdom. The wine ultimately speaks of the joy that the Holy Spirit brings into our lives when he fills us with His presence and His power.

VERSE 3

THE SHULAMITE (to her Beloved),

"Because of the fragrance of your good ointments,

Your name is ointment poured forth;

Therefore the virgins love you.

- *Ointment is symbolic of His loving acceptance.*

Fragrant ointments were very costly in Solomon's day. They were used for healing and for beautifying.

- *Fragrance is symbolic of the evidence of something.*

The name of Jesus is poured out on all mankind, and for those who receive and appropriate it, there is loving acceptance, beauty, and healing that will grace their lives throughout their journey through life. We see the teenagers of today falling prey to peer pressure because they crave acceptance. We all want and need acceptance because we were created that way. We were made in our Father's image and He wants us to accept Him. We never outgrow the need for acceptance.

Yes, Jesus accepts all who come to Him in His name for He is not willing that any should perish.

II Pet. 3:9 "The Lord is not slack concerning His promise, as some count slackness, but is long suffering toward us, not willing that any should perish but all should come to repentance." (NKJV)

When we accept Jesus into our lives, He gives us His name and we carry His name on our lives. We are betrothed to Him. We are accepted, we belong to Jesus! That craving for acceptance is met in Him! There is confidence that comes from belonging to Jesus, in knowing that we are accepted by the King of all kings. That confidence is the evidence (or fragrance) of His name on our lives and it is like ointment poured forth. That fragrance, Christian, will affect those around you just as His presence in the maiden's life has had an effect on the virgins in this verse. The virgins like the transformation that they see taking place in the Shulamite.

The "virgins" are more characters in the song. They are those who have not "...accepted other suitors in the world." But they have not yet accepted the King's contract of marriage either. They have not been born again, but they are open and seeking within the life of the church.

The virgins love the mention of His name and the promise of marriage, but they are not yet ready to invite Him into their lives and receive the joyful work of the Holy Spirit, which is the wine. You can read more about them in the parable of the wise and foolish virgins in Matthew 25.

What the Shulamite maiden is saying here to Solomon is this, "The virgins love You because they are beginning to see the evidence of the healing beauty that carrying Your name brings into my life." The maiden, at this point, is still dark with the effects of sin that remain on her life, as we will see in verse 5 of this chapter, but the King has given her His name upon sealing the contract of marriage. Having the assurance that she is loved and accepted by Him in spite of her present condition will continually work in her life to transform her as the effects of sin are washed away. We will see this transformation taking place in her throughout the song.

Maybe you are one who has heard the gospel message and you love everything about Jesus, but you have never asked Him into your life...you never accepted the salvation that Jesus offers to all those who will accept Him. You will not see or be a part of God's glorious kingdom or know what an intimate relationship with the King is like because you have not been born again. If that is the case, then let me encourage you, precious one, to set this book aside for a moment. Ask the Lord Jesus Christ to forgive you and make a decision to turn from your sinful ways. Ask Him to come into your life as Lord and Savior to live and reign from this day forward! Please do not put it off, for no one is guaranteed a tomorrow here on this Earth!!

John 3:3 Jesus answered and said the him, "Most assuredly, I say to you, unless one is born again, he cannot see the kingdom of God."

It is encouraging to realize that our Lord loves and accepts us even while we are yet still dark with the effects of sin, ignorant of His ways, and spiritually immature much like this maiden is at this point in the song. He loves and accepts us during every stage of the transformation that is taking place in us. It is His bridal love, the Prize that motivates us to move on through each phase of maturity to our destiny. This is just one more reason why it is so important for you, Christian, to study the Word so that you can know how God feels about you and how He sees you. Having the assurance that you are loved and accepted, in whatever state you are in, makes the administration of the Holy Spirit, who is at work in you, much easier and this transformation that we see taking place in the maiden of this song can take place in your own life as well!

King Solomon gave the Shulamite His name when she accepted the terms of His marriage contract. The Shulamite asked for His kisses in verse 1 of this chapter because she knew that she must have them in order to fulfill her part of the contract. His kisses, which are His instructions and discipline, received in an atmosphere of loving acceptance, are used by the Holy Spirit to do the joyful work in the maiden. The joy of the Holy Spirit at work in her and her determination to lay hold of the Prize will transform this humble maiden into a bride fit for a King and one that is ready to embrace her destiny in His kingdom.

VERSE 4

Draw me after you (away) and let us run together. (NAS)

Let the king bring me into his chambers. (NIV)

(The daughters of Jerusalem speak and say to the Shulamite)

We will be glad and rejoice in you.

(Then to the King)

We will remember your love more than wine.

(The Shulamite (speaks to her Beloved)

Rightly do they love you.

(Speaking of the daughters of Jerusalem)

The maiden makes three requests of the King here in this verse:

1. Draw me.
2. Let us run together.
3. Bring me into your chambers.

- *The drawing and the running are the heart of this song.*

Spending time in the King's chambers is where most of the transformation takes place in the maiden so that her life begins to produce a balance of the *drawing* and the *running.*

- *His chambers are the secret places where the couple share private intimate time together.*

- *Draw me away speaks of intimacy.*

This is the maiden's heart cry to know her King intimately. She longs to be an extravagant worshiper of God filled with a holy passion for her King.

From a practical point of view, what exactly are we talking about when we refer to "drawing apart" or that intimate time spent alone with Jesus? How does one do that and just exactly what can one expect to happen? Most importantly, what is there to gain from it?

The song talks much about drawing apart with the Bridegroom; that intimate time spent together in His chambers and of being in His embrace and receiving the kisses of his mouth. The whole song is presented within the context of a marriage between a man and a woman. In a marriage, when one desires to have intimate fellowship with his mate, he will set in motion a deliberate plan to create an atmosphere that the other person in the relationship cannot resist. He will set aside time to draw apart from the busy life just to spend time alone with his mate.

It works the same way if you, beloved, desire to spend intimate time with the Lord. Your comfortable living room or den might be the perfect setting for a time spent in the secret place of the King's chambers, or it may be outdoors under a tree with the natural praises of nature all around you.

From my own experience I have learned that the Lord cannot resist an atmosphere of praise! (**Ps 22:3**). For example, I put my favorite praise and worship CD on if I am at home, and I keep the Word of God at my fingertips in case He wants to speak to me from its pages. I prepare my heart for Him with self examination, confession, and repentance after I have settled myself into my favorite chair, then I wait before him as He fills my senses with His presence.

I may journal my thoughts after reading from my favorite devotion book or express my worship as I dance before Him. I may turn on my keyboard, write a love song and present it to Him or just sit at His feet (so to speak) and simply soak in His love.

This is a time to meditate on the Word/Jesus after receiving it; to seek understanding, wisdom, and knowledge of what I have been given. It is a time to rest in the Lord and to wait before Him, for the mysteries of God and all the treasures of wisdom and knowledge are hidden in Him, *and He is in us!*

> **Col. 1:27 ...this mystery among the Gentiles: which is Christ in you, the hope of glory. (NKJV)**

> **Col. 2:2-3 ...Christ, in Whom are hidden all the treasures of wisdom and knowledge. (NKJV)**

New life is the fruit born out of a time of intimacy in the King's chambers where one comes to know the King. It is the results of the drawing and of the running ... this is what you stand to gain!

Receiving the kisses of His mouth are the prerequisites to the impregnation of His word that is conceived in the King's chambers. This word (the word of God is also spoken of as a seed in the scriptures) is carried in one's spirit where it grows by the power of the Holy Spirit to maturity until it is birthed in ministry. This rhema word (rhema is a Greek word meaning "God's word as revealed by the Holy Spirit"), when it comes forth in ministry, brings spiritual rebirth and renewal into the lives of those who receive it. When this occurs, then more souls are birthed into the kingdom where they are nurtured and matured to a place in their walk where they begin to produce more fruit in like manner.

In terms of marriage, it is like a woman who has become pregnant with her husband's seed. She has received the seed into her womb (or spirit) where it remains for a period of time to be nurtured (meditation) and it grows there (understanding) until it is birthed as a new life (which is ministry of that word to others in knowledge and wisdom).

These words were spoken by the Apostle Paul in Ephesians within the context of marriage:

> **Eph. 5:32 This is a mystery but I speak concerning Christ and the church. (NKJV)**

I am always reluctant to end those special moments with my Lord and eager to make more time for Him the next day. I never fail to come away from those times encouraged, inspired, and empowered to run with *Him wherever He directs.*

- ***To run is to partner with the Bridegroom King in His work. It is obedience in action, at His unction, with a heart to minister to the needs of others.***

We have a picture of the *"drawing"* in the life of Mary, and the *"running"* in the life of Martha. Read Luke 10:38 and John 11:2.

Christians today need a balance in their lives of the two. We need to spend time in His presence in order to know Him more intimately and we also need to be ready to run with Him in ministry when He calls. One who is consumed with ministry to the exclusion of time apart spent in the Lord's presence in intimate fellowship many times experiences what we call physical and spiritual "burn out." They have become spiritually dry.

On the other hand, one who will not leave the King's chambers to share the truths they have received there, when He calls them to run in ministry with Him, is in danger of becoming a stagnant, stale pool of water going nowhere. A stagnant pool of water is a place that can breed all kinds of sickness and disease. Either extreme hinders useful service in the Kingdom of God.

This Shulamite knows about the King's chambers and she asks Him to carry her there where they will spend intimate, life changing time together. She knows that being in His presence will wash away all the darkness that is mentioned in the next verse from her life. This is a private place, a secret place, where she will learn this balance of drawing and running, among other things, and she longs for the day. It is here in these chamber experiences that the maiden's personal relationship with the King will develop and mature.

This secret place is mentioned in the Word numerous times. The Lord calls us today to join Him there for intimate fellowship! References to the secret place are found in:

> **Ps. 91:1, 4, 9-11**
> **Matt. 6:6**
> **Ps. 27:4-5**
> **Is. 45:3**

The daughters of Jerusalem are major characters in the song. They are those who have accepted the King's contract of marriage and are in various stages of maturity. The Holy Spirit is at work in them to prepare them for their wedding day. They are the Shulamite's support group because they are like-minded in their common goal. They are all after the Prize and they encourage one another to attain it. We will call them the bride company. Our maiden is now a part of this group and they are glad for the maiden. They rejoice with her as they remember their own chamber experiences with the King and they are renewed in their determination to gain the Prize.

The daughters of Jerusalem carry the rhema word from their own chamber experiences with the King as they run in ministry with the King and we see them ministering it to the maiden at the King's table in his banqueting house in chapter two of the song.

- *Remembrance*

There is something about remembrance that we do well to know. Remembrance stirs our passion. In this case it is our passion for Jesus that is stirred. Remembering will bring us back to our *first love* as referred to in Revelation.

> **Rev.2:4-5 Nevertheless I have this against you, that you have left your first love. Remember therefore from where you have fallen, repent and do the first works... (NKJV)**

In communion, when we drink the cup of wine, we are instructed to remember Jesus, and the passion for Him in our hearts is stirred.

> **I Cor. 11:25 In the same manner He also took the cup after supper saying, "This cup is the new covenant in My blood. This do, as often as you drink it, in remembrance of Me."**

In the last portion of this verse the maiden compares the love that the daughters of Jerusalem have for the King to the love the virgins have for Him and she says that the daughters of Jerusalem love Him in the right way.

"Do not look upon me because I am dark . . . ."
Song of Solomon 1:6

Karyl Simmons '05'

VERSE 5

I am dark but lovely,

O daughters of Jerusalem.

Like the tents of Kedar,

Like the curtains of Solomon.

- *Dark is symbolic of the effects of sin.*

- *Loveliness speaks of radiance, purity spotlessness and blamelessness.*

- *Tents were temporary houses for the nomad shepherds. They were made from the skins of wild goats and were grey or black in color.*

Kedar was one of twelve sons of Ishmael, the son of Abraham and the Egyptian servant girl, Hagar. The Arab peoples of today originated from these sons. Kedar was a nomad shepherd who dwelt in the desert of Arabia. Kedar literally means dark. You can find a description of these people in:

Gen. 16:12 He shall be a wild man, his hand shall be against every man and every man's against him. (NKJV)

The maiden compares her life to the tents of Kedar. The tents of Kedar speak of wild wandering with no roots, darkness (the effects of sin), obstinate and willful stubbornness (goats), and a disagreeable, mean-hearted personality. On the other hand, she compares her life to the curtains of Solomon which were white and made of fine linen.

- *White speaks of purity.*

- *Linen speaks of righteousness. (Rev 19:8)*

Solomon was a famous king of noble descent in the royal lineage of Jesus. He was the second son of David and Bathsheba and he was known for his wisdom. He wrote 3,000 proverbs and 1,000 songs. He authored Proverbs, Ecclesiastes, and the Song of Solomon. He was extremely wealthy and he possessed a great army with chariots and the finest horses. He loved women and maintained a harem of some 700 wives and 300 concubines.

It would seem that the maiden is contradicting herself with her remarks to the daughters of Jerusalem. This is what is called a paradox. The maiden is stating a fact here to the bride company. She realizes that she still carries the effects of sin on her life at this point in the song, but she then makes a statement of faith as well when she says, "But I am lovely."

This is to say, "I realize that I still carry the effects of sin on my life but I am now the righteousness of God in Christ Jesus and the Holy Spirit is at work in me, and I am becoming radiantly spotless and blamelessly pure. He has redeemed me from a life of dark wandering and strife to a life of royalty lived in peace and plenty."

Is. 60:1 Arise, shine, for your light has come! And the glory of the Lord is risen upon you. (NKJV)

- *The glory of the Lord is the beauty of this character.*

Saints of God, we have been redeemed in like manner, and the Holy Spirit is at work in us right now. He who has begun a good work in us is able to complete it.

Phil. 1:6 being confident of this very thing, that He who has begun a good work in you will complete it until the day of Jesus Christ. (NKJV)

When we accept Jesus, we know that His blood washes away our sin. The Word says it washes us as white as snow and we become the righteousness of God in Christ Jesus.

II Cor. 5:21 For He made Him who knew no sin to be sin for us, that we might become the righteousness of God in Him. (NKJV)

God, then, sees us from His point of view through the blood of Jesus. Because His blood covers us and washes us, He sees us as righteous. We, on the other hand, are seeing things from a different point of view.

Yes, we have accepted the righteousness of Christ by faith (which is the substance of things hoped for and the evidence of things not seen), but we are in a process; we are being changed from glory to glory as the effects of sin (which is the darkness the maiden speaks of) is being replaced with loveliness. This is sanctification!

The Shulamite maiden continues on in the next verse to confide in the daughters of Jerusalem the cause of her darkness.

VERSE 6

Do not look upon me because I am dark,

Because the sun has tanned me.

My mother's sons were angry with me,

They made me the keeper of the vineyards.

But my own vineyard I have not kept.

- *Sun is symbolic of Jesus, the Word.*

John 1:14
Matt.17:2
Ps. 19:4b-6
Ps. 84:11

In this case the Word was used out of context or legalistically (which is the Word minus the Spirit), and it was being misused by the Shulamite's brothers in order to benefit their own interests.

- *Vineyards are symbolic of the areas of one's interests and concerns.*

Her mother's sons would be the maiden's brothers. The brothers represent those men and women in the church who are religious, legalistic, and controlling. They are much like the Pharisees and Sadduccees of Jesus' day. They have deceived themselves into believing that they are doing God's work. They are making the maiden take care of areas of interest and responsibility that were not hers to do, causing her to neglect the areas for which she was responsible. They are angry with her because she is no longer under their control; she belongs to the King now.

You will see later in the song that these brothers are not balanced in the Word. They use the Word out of context to benefit their own interests. They are not at all concerned about how their selfish, abusive, controlling behavior affects those whom they dominate. The maiden was made to work in the heat of the day with no concern for her welfare and it had its sinful effects on her life. It must have caused great resentment, hurt, and bitterness in her heart toward her brothers. She was obviously ashamed for the bride company to see this darkness in her soul. These brothers are not necessarily false prophets or false teachers; they simply are not rightly dividing the Word. They are religious and not sincerely seeking God's presence to work change in their lives. They don't even realize that they need to change. They are steeped in legalism (which is the Word minus the revelations of the Holy Spirit).

The Shulamite's statement of faith in verse 5 intimidates these people who, up until now, have been able to dominate and control her. This maiden is beginning to break free of their influence and she is beginning to grow closer and stronger in her relationship to the King.

Have you ever encountered these brothers in your life song? They are still in the church today!

Before you think too harshly of the brothers, though, stop and think! Have you ever been in a position to behave like the maiden's brothers? We are all assigned to a flock to care for and sometimes there is a thin line between responsibly leading and protecting, and in controlling and dominating.

VERSE 7

(TO HER BELOVED)

Tell me, O you whom I love,

Where you feed your flock,

Where you make it rest at noon,

For why should I be as one who veils herself

By the flocks of your companions?

The Shulamite is seeing her beloved King now, as the Shepherd over a flock of which she is a part. This flock functions in an orderly and peaceful manner, according to the King's plan, and the maiden will learn servitude here in their midst.

> **I Cor. 14:33 For God is not the author of confusion** (disorder) **but of peace, as in all the churches of the saints. (NKJV)**
> **I Cor. 14:40 Let all things be done decently and in order. (NKJV)**

- *His flock represents those who serve as they follow Him.*

The maiden sees that her Beloved, the Shepherd King, leads His flock to good places to feed and drink. He protects His flock from harm and He cares for their needs. He makes His flock rest at noon. (Read Psalm 23)

The King's companions are part of His flock (those who serve as they follow Him). His companions stay very near the Shepherd King and are leaders that the King has placed within the flock. They are most likely the pastors, apostles, preachers, teachers, and evangelists of Ephesians 4:11 and I Corinthians 12. They are those in the church with the various ministries of healing, miracles, helps, administrations, etc. They have been given to the saints that are submissive to their authority to equip them for the work of the ministry and to build up the body of Christ.

> **Eph. 4:12 ...for the equipping of the saints for the work of ministry, for the edifying of the body of Christ. (NKJV)**

Each one in the King's flock has flocks as well whom they are responsible to serve. They are the body of Christ within the church – His hands, His feet, His voice to carry the gospel and minister to the needs of others, as they follow the Shepherd King. We will see in the next verse that the maiden has a flock to care for as do the King's companions mentioned in this verse. God has a purpose and a perfect plan for each of us and we must walk in it, God's way! If all in the Shepherd's flock are functioning according to His plan, they will learn how to serve effectively while under God's protective authority. They will also learn how to serve as a protective authority over others in the flock while they are maturing in servitude.

Compared to the maiden's abusive brothers who made her work through the hottest part of the day out in the scorching sun with no concern for her welfare, this is a wonderful revelation of her Bridegroom King and it makes her aware of how much she is beginning to love Him. She is eager to mature so that she can take her place as His bride-queen. She wants to eat her spiritual food directly from His hand and she questions why she cannot feed nearer to Him. After all, she is His bride-elect! We can see here a glimpse of the darkness, the willful stubbornness, that she confessed to the bride company in verse 5 of this chapter. But she is hungry to grow in knowledge and to mature so that she can lay hold of the Prize.

What she must realize, though, is that there are no spoiled brats in the bride company and there are no short cuts for the bride! She must learn to do things God's way.

Now, what is this veil that the maiden refers to here in the last part of this verse?

A young woman in ancient Jewish tradition, when she agreed to a contract of marriage, would wear a veil when out in public. The veil, in honor of the contract, was a sign to all other potential suitors that she was spoken for and not available for marriage to any of the other young men. It was much like an engagement ring that young women wear today.

- ***The veil in this verse symbolizes the maiden's witness to the world that she belongs to the King.***

It represents her commitment to serve Him and His interests alone; that she will keep herself pure for Him alone, and that she will allow the Holy Spirit to prepare her to take her place as His bride-queen. Her veil covers and protects her from the influences of the world that would pull her away from her focus, and her determination to lay hold of the Prize. It seals the maiden's body for the King alone.

This is speaking of the maiden's lifestyle – a life style of servitude and righteousness. In verse 2 of chapter 1, the maiden's soul was sealed. We are a spirit that possesses a soul and lives in a body and here, her body is sealed or certified, not to be tampered with, unto righteousness and servitude.

> **II Thess. 5:23-24 Now may the God of peace Himself sanctify you completely, and may your whole spirit, soul, and body be preserved blameless at the coming of our Lord Jesus Christ. He who calls you is faithful, who also will do it. (NKJV)**

VERSE 8

THE BELOVED

If you do not know,

O fairest among women,

Follow in the footsteps of the flock

And feed your little goats

Beside the Shepherd's tents.

- ***Goats are symbolic of those who are willful, stubborn, and disobedient. They are in need of someone to disciple them. (Matt 25:31-46)***

- ***Shepherds are those who are committed to the care of those assigned to them.***

- ***Tents speak of mobility and in this context, a heart to follow after God.***

The shepherds, in their servitude, go to where the need is. They go and they lead their flocks into God's presence, and where there is food for them.

- ***Fair means beautiful or unveiled. Unveiled speaks of transparency, vulnerability, and availability.***

- ***To follow speaks of submissive obedience.***

The beloved Shepherd King speaks now for the first time in the song. He is telling her, in response to her obstinate question, that if you do not know why I require you to take your place in the flock before you can move on to your destiny, and if you want to know, then submit yourself to the godly authority that I have placed over you (the shepherds) and learn from the experienced wisdom of those in my flock who have learned to serve as they follow Me.

> **John 12: 26 "If anyone serves Me, let him follow Me, and where I am, there shall My servant also be, if anyone serves Me, the Father will honor him." (NAS)**

Notice that even at this early stage in her transformation, the King refers to her as *fairest among women.* In her vulnerable transparency before Him, He calls her beautiful even though her attitude is one of obstinate, stubborn, willfulness. He is seeing, instead, the finished work in her.

In verse 4 of this chapter, the Shulamite asked to run with the King, which is to partner in ministry with her Beloved, but she must receive spiritual nurturing and training in the body of Christ before she is ready to do this. Being trained and fed God's way offers her protection from the influences of the world while she learns these lessons in servitude.

This is also a lesson for her in obedience to God's ordained, delegated authority; how to function under it in order to get her needs met and how to learn to be that godly authority over her flock, the little goats, as she ministers to their needs and disciples them.

The maiden has been given the King's kisses of instruction that she asked for in verse 2.

It is so important for us as Christians to realize that one of the enemy's most effective tactics against us is to isolate us from the body of Christ. If you are effectively serving and growing in the body, then you are a big threat to him! If the enemy can pull you away from your protection, then he is better able to trip you up. He will even attempt to destroy you, if you allow it.

> **John 10:10 "The thief does not come except to steal, and to kill, and to destroy. I have come that they may have life, and that they may have it more abundantly." (NKJV)**

There is a great temptation among Christians today who have had a bad experience within the life of the church to withdraw and isolate themselves. Many fall away completely from their walk with the Lord.

Did you know that there is a scientific law that states that when things are isolated, they tend to deteriorate? There is no such thing as a perfect church! After all, the church is made of people like you and me and I will be the first to say that I am far from perfect.

In I Cor 11:27-29 we are instructed, when taking communion, to examine ourselves first, and discern the body of Christ before eating the bread representing Jesus' body and drinking the wine representing His blood. The church is one of our Lord's primary interests and therefore, our interest as well. There, we are to serve His interests as He directs.

> **I Cor. 11:27-29 Therefore whoever eats this bread or drinks this cup of the Lord in an unworthy manner will be guilty of the body and blood of the Lord. But let a man examine himself and so let him eat of this bread and drink of the cup. For he who eats and drinks in an unworthy manner eats and drinks judgment to himself, not discerning the Lord's body. (NKJV)**

Remember this! Finding our place in the body of Christ is what God has purposed for us in order to bring us to our destiny with Him. Taking our place there is like accepting the veil and wearing it so that all the world will know that we belong to Jesus and will serve Him all the days of our lives. He just may be saying to you that if you want Me to feed and satisfy you, then you must find My purposes for you in the body of Christ within the church and follow in the footsteps of the flock!

This is the first of four tests for the maiden...will she pass it?

VERSE 9

I have compared you, my love,

To my filly among Pharoah's chariots.

- *A filly is a young, fit, energetic, strong, and beautiful female horse. A filly would also be inexperienced and untrained, but eager to run.*

This lovely animal must be broken and trained so that it can be guided with a bit and reins in order to be useful to the King. Many times they are stubborn and strong willed which are good traits in a horse when brought under the subjection and control of its master. This would be what is referred to as a spirited filly.

- *Chariots are horse drawn vehicles used in warfare by the Pharoahs of Egypt.*

The King sees the same traits in this Shulamite maiden that He sees in His filly. This maiden will be trained for warfare before this song is ended, as we will soon discover.

Look for the bride of Christ, beloved, in these perilous last days, to be trained and ready for spiritual warfare.

Notice the King refers to the Shulamite here as "My love," speaking of His love for her even though she is inexperienced, untrained and strong willed much like the flock she is to care for – the goats.

VERSE 10

Your cheeks are lovely with ornaments,

Your neck with chains of gold.

- *Cheeks are symbolic of emotions. It speaks of the heart's affections.*

- *Ornaments symbolize her acceptance.*

Ornaments were a part of the bride price in the marriage contract that the prospective groom offered to the prospective bride. In this case they were probably earrings. Genesis 23:22 and 29 talks about this in the account of Isaac, his servant and Rebekah. These ornaments speak of her born again experience; her acceptance of Jesus into her life.

- *Gold is symbolic of God's diving nature.*

- *Chains are symbolic of authority.*

These chains are like the bits and reins the King would use to train a filly so that he could guide her.

- *The neck is symbolic of the will.*

We see the Shulamite here in this verse wearing the ornaments. In wearing the ornaments, the maiden is showing to all that she has accepted the King and his kisses of instruction and discipline, and that she has placed her heart's affections on Him alone. She is wearing the gold chains as well, which says to all, "I have also accepted the Godly authority that you have asked me to submit myself to (which are the God-ordained leaders in the body of Christ), and I will learn to embrace servanthood, God's way, by an act of my will." The maiden has accepted the veil and she will wear it as a witness to all the world of her commitment to her beloved bridegroom King.

Yes, the Shulamite maiden has passed the first test! How about you, Christian?

VERSE 11

THE DAUGHTERS OF JERUSALEM

(speak and say to the maiden)

We will make you ornaments of gold

With studs of silver.

- *Gold speaks of God's divine nature.*

- *Ornaments speak of acceptance.*

- *Silver speaks of redemption.*

These ornaments may have been a crown, bracelets, rings, or earrings; notice that they are all *circles*.

- *Circles speak of unending love, much like the rings that are exchanged in a wedding ceremony today.*

The bride company wants the Shulamite to accept their encouragement to help her to remember that the love of the Beloved for the bride is unconditional and unending. His love produces God's divine nature in her life, and that His sacrificial love has paid the price to redeem her from the dark bondages of her past.

Dear one, do you take the initiative to encourage other Christians to reach for the goal of the prize as the daughters of Jerusalem are encouraging the maiden here in this verse?

This verse is a picture of *discipleship*. We have all been commanded to go and make disciples of all nations, and each of us has a flock that we are to disciple. If we will all follow God's plan, then the whole world will have an opportunity to be saved!

VERSE 12

THE SHULAMITE

While the King is at his table

My spikenard sends forth its fragrance.

- *Spikenard is symbolic of praise and worship.*

Spikenard is a spice. It was a very costly and fragrant oil used in perfume and ointments of Solomon's day.

- *Spices are symbolic of the various administrations of the Holy Spirit in one's life.*

- *Fragrance is the evidence of something.*

The Shulamite has taken her place in the King's flock and is submitted to the authority of the shepherds as she is being trained in servitude. But, what she really longs for is to be in a more intimate setting near her King at his table and to be fed by His hand. She is not satisfied to just be in His flock, feeding with the others near the shepherds' tents.

Her focus remains on Him and the prize. She sees Him at His table where she longs to be and she begins to praise Him and her worship begins to fill the atmosphere where He is. This scene is repeated in

John 12:1-2 while Jesus was reclining at a table in the home of Lazarus. While Martha served, Mary began to pour out a very expensive container of spikenard on the feet of Jesus and the house was filled with the fragrance of the perfume. Lazarus was at the table of the King where the maiden of this song longs to be. She eventually finds herself there in the next chapter but note in verse 9-11 of this account in John that the chief priests were plotting to kill not only the King, but Lazarus as well. They wanted Lazarus dead because his life was a living witness of Jesus' resurrection power and many were following Jesus because of his testimony. This situation was causing the priests to lose control over the people...sound familiar?

Ps. 23:5 You prepare a table before me in the presence of my enemies. You anoint my head with oil. (NKJV)

Here in these verses from the Gospel of John, we are finding more insight into the brothers of the song.

Beware of the brothers, Christian, in your own life's song for they will attempt to stifle the life of Jesus in your life and the effects it has on those around you. They are those whom the brothers have previously been able to manipulate and control to their own advantage.

The maiden's praise and worship is evidenced by a fragrance that rises before the King; a fragrance that He cannot ignore or resist. True praise and worship is a work of the Holy Spirit in one's life. God is seeking true worshipers today and He inhabits their praises.

John 4:23 "But the hour is coming, and now is, when the true worshipers will worship the Father in spirit and truth; for the Father is seeking such to worship Him." (NKJV)

Ps. 22:3 But you are holy, enthroned in the praises of Israel. (NKJV)

Why do you think that God seeks our worship? Well, worship is love and adoration. The very things we need from God, he needs from us! We are made in His image and we have the same basic needs that He has. Our praise and worship creates an atmosphere that our Beloved will inhabit. It invites His presence into our circumstances where we can connect and minister to one another.

Christian, are you able to lift true and sincere praise and worship to the Lord in the midst of hard circumstances, especially when you do not seem to receive the answers to your prayers that you desire in a timely manner? Let us take a valuable lesson from the maiden and learn from her example in this verse. This is what the Bible refers to as a *sacrifice of praise.*

Heb. 13:15 ...let us continually offer the sacrifice of praise to God, that is, the fruit of our lips, giving thanks to His name. (NKJV)

True praise and worship will lift you above your circumstances and place you in His presence where you will find strength and comfort in His embrace.

I would like to take the liberty to share a poem that I was inspired by the Holy Spirit to pen several years ago after seeing this in a vision.

Praise Takes You There

By Karyl Simmons

Close your eyes for just a moment and still the hands of time.
Behold a golden temple in the quietness of your mind.
Ornate doors swing open wide as a glorious sight unfolds,
And all of heaven watches as the King descends his throne.
How many times you've wondered how this event would be,
Your eyes beholding Jesus – to feel, to touch, to see.
You marvel at the beauty this dwelling place commands,
Yet fading in all its glory now, as Christ before you stands.
His eyes, they see right through you. This One knows you well.
He doesn't speak a single word, there's nothing left to tell.
For all the truth you've sought to know is found in this one life
The one who died that you might live, this man named Jesus Christ.
And the glorious beauty that enthrones Him is created by one thing;
Your praising heart that lifts Him up and loves Him as you sing.
Did you know that He sings? He's rejoicing over you
Joining his voice with your voice and the angels' voices, too.
It's a great big hallelujah time as you dance around together
You laugh, He laughs – rapturous joy that lasts forever.
So keep this thought for always in the recesses of your mind,
And recall it often, child of God, and you'll delight to find
That praise will always take you there, to wondrous sights unknown,
And place you gently, every time, before His glorious throne.
All your needs are met right there before His mercy seat,
And all the truth that heaven holds, you'll find at Jesus' feet.

VERSE 13

A bundle of myrrh is my beloved to me

That lies all night between my breasts.

- *Myrrh is symbolic of suffering love.*

Myrrh is a spice therefore it is another work of the Holy Spirit in one's life. Myrrh in ancient times was very costly and was used in embalming and to beautify. It was sweet smelling and very soothing and healing. It was given to Jesus as a drink when He was on the cross.

- *Night speaks of suffering through a dark, hard time.*

- *Between my breasts is a phrase that speaks of embracing.*

The Shulamite is saying in her praise and worship to her Beloved that she is learning to embrace His suffering love through this dark, hard time in her life.

What is it to embrace His suffering love? It is putting someone else's need above your own need, comfort, or desires because you love Jesus and because the Holy Spirit has directed you to do so. It is dying to self and crucifying your fleshly desires in sacrificial love for someone else with a peace that passes all human understanding. It is loving those who persecute you or treat you badly (someone like the brothers in this song, for instance) with the joy of the Lord strengthening you to do so.

It is hiding yourself in your Beloved's embrace and holding on to Him and enjoying His presence during the dark, hard times and staying there until it passes.

The ultimate example of suffering love is Jesus on the cross. It is a work of the Holy Spirit in one's life. The cross that was in Jesus' day a symbol if suffering and certain death and that was most feared has now become a symbol of life and hope because Jesus willingly and obediently chose to embrace suffering on that cross. He did it out of His love for you and me and out of His love for His Father. The Father knew that we needed someone to rescue us from sin and death, so he sent Jesus to take our sin on the cross in order that we could walk free of it into abundant life with Him. In doing so, He conquered Satan and death on that cross. Jesus is my hero and a Man among men.

To embrace suffering love is a choice one makes. Read the words of Jesus, as recorded in the Gospel of Matthew when the soldiers came to arrest Him while He was praying in the garden:

> **Matt. 26:53 "Or do you think that I cannot now pray to My Father and He will provide Me with more than twelve legions of angels?" (NKJV)**

In like manner, Christian, if you will choose to embrace suffering when it comes, rather than fear it, or think to avoid it, you will find freedom from Satan's chains – freedom to live the abundant life that the Father meant all along for you to have.

> **II Tim. 3:12 Yes, and all who desire to live Godly in Christ Jesus will suffer persecution. (NKJV)**

> **Rom. 8:16-17 The Spirit Himself bears witness with our spirit that we are children of God, and if children, then heirs – heirs of God and joint heirs with Christ, if indeed we suffer with Him, that we may also be glorified together.**

> **I Pet. 2:20b-21 But when you do good and suffer, if you take it patiently, this is commendable before God. For to this you were called, because Christ also suffered for us, leaving us an example, that you should follow His steps. (NKJV)**

Suffering, at some point in one form or another, is a given in a person's life and Christians are not exempt. The thought of facing those dark, hard times used to frighten me until I learned to face them from my Beloved's embrace (much like the Shulamite is learning to do here). I am discovering peace in His arms, in the midst of those hard times and Satan has lost his stronghold in my life – that stronghold was the fear of those dark, hard times.

You will remember that the maiden's soul was sealed by the Holy Spirit to God not to be tampered with. If you belong to Jesus, Satan has no authority to tamper with you. One of his many weapons is fear and when you, child of God, eliminate fear from your life by replacing it with faith and trust in your Beloved's ability to save you, you disarm the enemy of your soul of that weapon.

VERSE 14

My beloved is to me a cluster of henna blooms

In the vineyards of En Gedi

- *Vineyards is symbolic of one's interests or concerns.*

- *Henna blooms speak of being transformed into His (Jesus) image.*

These flowers were used by Jewish maidens for adornment in Solomon's day. Their leaves produced a dye that the people of that day would use cosmetically to color their hair and beards.

En Gedi is a beautiful, refreshing oasis in a harsh, dry desert place in Israel. It is in the Judean desert and is a place where David would go many times in order to hide from King Saul as recorded in the Old Testament.

In this verse, the Shulamite is saying, in her praise and worship, "My Beloved has become my adornment and He has transformed my life so that I am able to delight myself in Him and His interests even though I am in a hard, dry, barren place."

Gal. 3:27 For as many of you as were baptized into Christ have put on Christ. (NKJV)

She has learned to hide herself in Him during times of trouble.

Ps. 32:7 You are my hiding place, You shall preserve me from trouble, You shall surround me with songs of deliverance. (NKJV)

Col. 3:3 For you died and your life is hidden with Christ in God. (NKJV)

Yes, the King's love for you, beloved Christian, can refresh you and grace your life with beauty, even during those hard, dark times. Jesus is that safe refuge – that place you can run to in times of trouble.

VERSE 15

THE BELOVED

Behold, you are fair, my love!

Behold, you are fair.

You have dove's eyes.

- *Fair means beautiful and unveiled. Unveiled speaks of transparency, vulnerability, and availability.*

The Beloved responds to the Shulamite's praise and worship by affirming and then reaffirming to her just how beautiful she is to Him in her worship. Her beauty is in her transparency and her vulnerability to Him. We are instructed in I Chr. 16:29 to worship the Lord in the beauty of holiness. Transparency and vulnerability before God is a prerequisite to holiness.

Any time the maiden is before the King, she is unveiled and available to Him. You will remember that the maiden wears the veil when she is out in public to discourage other suitors.

The Beloved is saying to this Shulamite, "Look at you, just look at you! You are beautiful!" He then refers to her again as "My love."

Every woman (including myself) I have ever known cries out, in one way or another, to be known by someone, anyone, as beautiful. Men and women long for acceptance, admiration, affirmation, and approval. Did you know that God, in his wonderful wisdom, made all that way? That need in our lives is what He uses to draw us to Him because He is the One who can truly fulfill that longing deep inside us! Many of us have spent a lifetime looking in all the wrong places to have that need met, but it is met only in Jesus!

The King then admires the maiden's eyes and refers to them as dove's eyes.

- *Doves can focus on only one thing at a time.*

The maiden's eyes are focused on her Beloved and on Him alone while she walks through this hard time of her life. Her ability to stay focused on Him as she worships her King draws His admiration.

VERSE 16

THE SHULAMITE

Behold, you are handsome, my beloved!

Yes, pleasant!

Also our bed is green.

The Shulamite in the previous verses of this chapter has asked for the King's kisses. She has:

♦Expressed an appreciation for His name.

♦Expressed a desire to know Him better.

♦Expressed her appreciation to Him for the benefits that knowing Him is bringing into her life in worship.

Now suddenly, she realizes how very attractive He has become to her and how very much she enjoys His company. She feels safe and comfortable with Him. This Shulamite is beginning to fall in love with the King! She has begun to express ownership of Him when she refers to Him as "my Beloved," and in so doing, fills His greatest longing to be loved and adored.

- *Bed speaks of rest.*

- *Green speaks of lushness, health, and life.*

The Shulamite has discovered that since she has submitted her will to Him and stopped striving in her flesh, she has found a rest in Him that produces a lushness of life and health even in this dark, hard time.

Christian, this is a discovery that would grace your own life's song with a peace that would pass all understanding if you would learn it from this maiden's own experience. Stress is the opposite of peace. Stress will destroy your peace and, if not handled properly, it will destroy your health. We must learn how to enter into His rest.

Heb. 4:9-10 There remains therefore as rest for the people of God. For he who has entered his rest has himself also ceased from his works as God did from His. (NKJV)

Matt. 11:28 "Come to me, all you who labor and are heavy laden, and I will give you rest." (NKJV)

Phil. 4:7 and the peace of God, which surpasses all understanding, will guard your hearts and minds through Christ Jesus. (NKJV)

VERSE 17

The beams of our houses are cedar

And our rafters of fir.

- *Beams and rafters are structural components in a house.*

- *Houses speaks of one's body.*

- *Cedar is symbolic of the righteousness of the new creation.*

- *Fir is symbolic of death.*

In essence, what the Shulamite is saying in her worship of the King is that becoming a new creation who is righteous in God's eyes and dying to the old man while in this body are structural truths that she can build upon now that they are set in place. The Shulamite can now grow into the spiritual maturity that she desires for her life. She is determined to lay hold of the Prize!

II Cor. 5:17 Therefore if anyone is in Christ, he is a new creation; old things have passed away, behold all things have become new. (NKJV)

CHAPTER ONE REVIEW

1. What does the Song of Solomon represent? _____

_____

2. In the context of this study, what does it mean to receive His kisses?

_____

3. There are two things that wine symbolizes. What are they? _____

_____

4. In the context of this study, whom do the Shulamite's brothers represent? _____

_____

5. Willfully disobedient and stubborn people are represented by what? _____

_____

6. What does Solomon mean when he compares the Shulamite to a filly? _____

_____

7. When the Shulamite wears the ornaments, what is she saying? _____

_____

8. What is unusual about doves' eyes? _____

_____

9. One's interests and concerns are represented by what? _____

_____

10. In the context of this study, what is the Prize? _____

_____

CHAPTER TWO

THE EMBRACE

VERSE 1

I am the rose of Sharon

And the lily of the valleys.

- *The rose of Sharon is a common, ordinary flower in Israel.*

You can see them all along the countryside. They are very hardy and plentiful. Less plentiful is the lily of the valleys.

- *The lily of the valleys is symbolic of the Bride of Christ.*

This is the bride who struggles with compromise, indifference and complacency (the valley).

In chapter 1 verse 5, the Shulamite maiden confesses that she is dark and then she makes a statement of faith when she says that she is lovely. Now, in this verse, she states another fact: *she is common and ordinary and that there are many others like her.* She then makes her second statement of faith when she says she is the *lily of the valleys.* She is saying, "I am the bride of Christ even though I surely do not look like it right now, for I am struggling with compromise, indifference, and complacency. However, I have determined to gain the Prize."

Meditate on these scriptures for a while:

> **Matt. 7:14 ... narrow is the gate and difficult is the way which leads to life and there are few who find it. (NKJV)**

> **Matt. 22:14 ...for many are called but few are chosen. (NKJV)**

Dear one, will you be one of those who will press on until you lay hold of the Prize? Will you strive to fulfill your destiny and take your place beside the King in God's Kingdom as His glorious Bride-Queen, even though you are a common, ordinary servant of God that struggles sometimes in the valley of compromise, indifference, and complacency?

I have observed from the Word and from my own experience that the company of those who are seeking a more intimate relationship with the Lord gets smaller and smaller the closer they get to Him. Not only does the company of people grow smaller, but the individuals, themselves, grow smaller or less dominant in the relationship as one becomes more and more like Him.

> **John 3:29-30 "He who has the bride is the bridegroom; but the friend of the bridegroom, who stands and hears him, rejoices greatly because of the bridegroom's voice. Therefore this joy of mine is fulfilled. 30: "He must increase, but I must decrease.**

Christian, will you allow these truths from God's Word to strengthen your determination to have all that He has purposed for you, even when the path gets narrow and hard, and those who travel it with you become fewer?

VERSE 2

THE BELOVED

Like a lily among thorns

So is my love among the daughters.

- *Lily is symbolic of the Bride-Queen.*

- *Thorns are symbolic of the sinful, cursed earth.*

- *Daughters are referring to all other women of the world.*

Again, the Beloved is speaking words of affirmation over His bride. Notice that the bride's statements of faith in the previous verses are in agreement with what the King says about her, except for her reference to the valleys. The King is seeing the completed work of the Holy Spirit in her in spite of her struggles.

The King is saying here, "My love, My bride, who is pursuing the promise of the Prize, stands out in stark contrast from all the other women of the world who are living on this sinful, cursed earth."

I heard someone say once that having Jesus in your life doesn't make you perfect, but it does make you different. God says in I Pet. 2:9 that you are chosen, you are royal, you are holy, and you are special (or peculiar).

Every ordinary man or woman of God in this world has the extraordinary promises of God offered to them, but they must determine to embrace and walk in those promises if they are to gain the Prize. This is what makes you different or peculiar to all others – you are living in this world, but you have a Heavenly goal in sight. You are after the Prize!

But be aware that your enemy, Satan, the father of all lies and the god of this world, will attempt to deceive anyone who has determined to embrace the promises of God. He wants to prevent you, child of God, from walking in those promises because he would like to make God look like a liar and His Word seem of no effect. We know, though, that God cannot lie and that His Word is powerful.

Heb. 6:18 ...that by two immutable things, in which it is impossible for God to lie, ... (NKJV)

John 8:44 "You are of your father the devil, and the desires of your father you want to do. He was a murderer from the beginning, and does not stand in the truth, because there is no truth in him. When he speaks a lie, he speaks from his own resources, for he is a liar and the father of it." (NKJV)

Satan would also like to make you feel like a failure in order to discourage you from pursuing the Prize. But God says that you can do all things through Christ who strengthens you as mentioned in Philippians 4:13.

Deception is another weapon that Satan will use to trip us up as we run the race. Knowing, understanding, and doing the Word will disarm the enemy of this weapon, as the maiden will soon discover.

VERSE 3

THE SHULAMITE

Like an apple tree among the trees of the woods

So is my beloved among the sons.

I sat down in his shade with great delight

And his fruit was sweet to my taste.

- *The apple tree represents Jesus.*

An apple tree in the woods stands out from all other trees because it provides fruit that nourishes everyone who eats of it.

- *Trees of the woods represent all humanity.*

- *The sons represent all other men in the world.*

- *Sat down speaks of rest from all physical activity.*

- *His shade is His protection from the effects of sin.*

You will remember that the brothers used the word legalistically (with no revelation of the Holy Spirit) against their sister. They made her work out in the heat of the day, causing her to be dark with the effects of sin.

- *His fruit is His revealed truth.*

They are the apples mentioned in verse 5 of this chapter.

The Shulamite sees her Beloved as superior to all other men of all time. There is just no one like Jesus. She looks to her Beloved for her nurturing, for protection, and for truth. Jesus said in John 14:6 "...I am the way, the truth, and the life..." His way offers us protection and His truth (which is His fruit) nurtures and sustains His life in us,

The maiden rests from her labor under His shade with great delight, and she begins to nibble on His revealed truth. This is delightful to her because she, no doubt, is remembering how she was made to labor for her brothers out in the heat of the day with no concern for her welfare. This is a step closer for her to His table and nearer to Him where she longs to be, feeding on the Word straight from His hand.

These truths and His great love for her are lifting her up out of her ugly circumstances and they are washing away the effects of sin (the darkness of her soul). They are sweet to her because they nurture and strengthen her spirit.

Ps. 119:103 How sweet are Your words to my taste, sweeter than honey to my mouth. (NKJV)

When was the last time that you, beloved, took the time from your active lives to rest under Jesus' shade and to nibble on His revealed truths?

VERSE 4

THE SHULAMITE TO THE DAUGTHTERS OF JERUSALEM

He brought me to the banqueting house,

And his banner over me was love.

- *Brought, in this case, is to carry.*

In chapter 3 we will see Solomon's couch or palanquin that carries the maiden to her wedding day. It is a portable chair that is carried on the shoulders of valiant men. We will discover that this palanquin represents our faith in God and His Word and the Gospel message of Jesus.

- *The banqueting house is a public or corporate setting of the church, a gathering place where those present are offered food from His table.*

Ps. 23:5 You prepare a table before me in the presence of my enemies. You anoint my head with oil, my cup runs over. (NKJV)

- *His banner of love identifies those who have determined to gain the Prize.*

A banner in ancient times was raised as a rallying point for groups with a common interest. Many times it was a signal to call an army to assemble together for battle.

In this verse, I believe the banner lifted over the Shulamite maiden and the other daughters of Jerusalem identifies them in this corporate setting of the church as the bride company. They have rallied together under this banner of love and have made a proclamation to all there that they have determined to gain the Prize. Furthermore, they have purposed in their hearts to defeat the enemy who would attempt to keep them from reaching their goal.

The Shulamite turns to her support group and proclaims, "The King has carried me into the banqueting house and to a place at His table with you."

In meditating on this verse and thinking about the banqueting house, I began to reflect on how many times in the scriptures Jesus was concerned about, or involved in, feeding people and giving them physical, but more importantly, spiritual food. That God's people feed on the Word and drink in the Living Water is much more important to the Father than I think we realize.

> **John 4:14 "but whoever drinks of the water that I shall give him will never thirst. But the water that I shall give him will become in him a fountain of water springing up into everlasting life." (NKJV)**

> **John 6:27 "Do not labor for the food which perishes, but for the food which endures to everlasting life, which the Son of Man will give you..." (NKJV)**

> **Prov. 4:20-22 My son, give attention to my words, incline your ear to my sayings. Do not let them depart from your eyes, keep them in the midst of your heart, for they are life to those who find them, and health to all their flesh. (NKJV)**

Jesus told Peter to feed His sheep in John 21:15-17; He fed the 4,000 in John 4; He prepared breakfast for Peter and the other disciples by the seashore after His resurrection in John 21:1-14, and in Psalm 23:5 He prepared a table for me!

In this song alone, there are numerous references to feasting on the rhema word.

Let us now see what transpires in the maiden's life as she finds herself at the King's table in the banqueting house. I believe at the end of this study we will fully understand the importance of God's rhema word in the life of a Christian.

The Shulamite expressed her desire to be carried into the King's chambers in chapter 1, verse 4. She was given instruction and correction (His kisses) that she must follow in order to prepare herself to eventually take her place as the King's bride in His Kingdom. She made her statements of faith in verse 1:5 and in verse 2:1 and she set her heart's affections and her focus on Him alone. She found rest under His shade as she tasted of His revealed truths, all the while longing to be nearer to Him and to be fed at His table.

Now her faith in God has carried her into the banqueting house and to His table where she has joined the other members of the bride company under his banner, proclaiming to all who are there that she belongs exclusively to Jehovah Nissi as He places His banner of love over her. Jehovah Nissi is one of the Hebrew names of God meaning "my banner."

The ordinary Shulamite shepherd girl glories in the fact that she is finally at the King's table where she saw Him in chapter 1. She had longed to be at his table as she worshipped Him. Now she is rallied around His banner of love with the rest of the bride company, a runner in the race with those who have determined to gain the Prize!

VERSE 5

Sustain me with cakes of raisins.

Refresh me with apples

For I am lovesick.

- *Cakes of raisins are symbolic of the solid food of the Word.*

Raisins are dried grapes. Grapes are the fruit of the vine (the church). These cakes of raisins are the solid food of the Word and they are offered to her through the administration and the auspices of the church.

- *Apples symbolize the revelation of truth from the Word by the Holy Spirit.*

Do you remember the little shepherdess back in chapter 1, verse 7, who wanted so much just to feed near the Shepherd King – the humble maiden who saw Him at His table and worshiped in verse 12? Well, now she is not only at His table and next to Him, but she is in His embrace! You will see in the next verse that she is drinking in the administrations of the Holy Spirit as the bride company serves her the solid food of the Word. This rhema word refreshes her spirit with truth that is revealed by the Holy Spirit who is at work in her. In Matt. 7:7 Jesus promises that all those who seek will find!

Her Beloved has prepared a table for her in the presence of her enemies. All are there in the church (including her brothers), and she is overcome with a holy passion for Him. She is lovesick! Feasting on His rhema word has this effect on our lives.

> **Ps. 23:5 You prepare a table for me in the presence of my enemies. (NKJV)**

Who are her enemies? Her enemies are those who would kill the work of the Holy Spirit in her life – in this case, they are her brothers and they are still in the church today.

Do not be discouraged, Christian, when you encounter the brothers in your life's song, and do not be dismayed when you find them in the life of the church. Remember that Judas was one of the twelve disciples who walked with Jesus and he was a part of God's plan in the lives of the other disciples.

I must say again that the church today is not perfect because it is made up of imperfect people like you and me. But the church is part of God's plan for your life. Satan would love to isolate you from that place where God has purposed for you to serve and mature. He does not want you to have the Prize! He does not want you to find your place in the Kingdom and move into your destiny.

When we have been in the manifested presence of the Lord, it can leave us physically exhausted or as in this verse, lovesick. Jesus reveals Himself little by little and we are changed from glory to glory or we could not bear it.

> **John 16:12 "I still have many things to say to you, but you cannot bear them now." (NKJV)**

Ps. 39:13 "Remove your gaze from me, that I may regain my strength, before I go away and am no more." (NKJV)

His left hand is under my head and His right hand embraces me.
Song of Solomon 2:6

VERSE 6

His left hand is under my head,

And his right hand embraces me.

This is an intimate picture of the Beloved with the Shulamite that we will see two other times in the song. Here they are in a corporate setting of the church. They are in the banqueting house reclining at His table. She has been feeding on the solid food of the Word and Revelation Truth.

- *Now his left hand is under her head. This speaks of the renewing of her mind.*

- *His right hand embraces her as He captures her heart's affections.*

She is resting in His arms as she meditates on the rhema Word that she has just been fed and she is beginning to know Him more intimately. You will remember in the previous verse feasting on the rhema Word has caused her to be lovesick and now the King is capturing her heart's affections.

Never hesitate, beloved, to draw apart to spend time in this embrace. While you are there, ask the Holy Spirit to bring revelation to you as you feed upon the solid food of the Word. You will soon find that your mind will be renewed and you will discover a holy passion for Jesus in your life as He captures your heart's affections.

I Cor. 2:13 These things we also speak, not in words which man's wisdom teaches but which the Holy Spirit teaches, comparing spiritual things with spiritual. (NKJV)

VERSE 7

I charge you, O daughters of Jerusalem,

By the gazelles or by the does of the field

Do not stir up nor awaken love

Until it pleases.

- *Gazelle is symbolic of the resurrected Jesus who has overcome. It is speaking of the Bridegroom King of the song.*

- *Does of the field is symbolic of the gazelle's hungry partner. It is speaking of the maiden in the song.*

This hungry maiden has just feasted on the raisin cakes. She has taken in the rhema Word that was ministered to her by the bride company. The King is now holding her in His embrace as He renews her mind with that Word. He is capturing her heart's affections as her eyes are focused on Him alone. She is, no doubt, receiving more of His kisses which are His instruction and discipline or correction.

The maiden has longed for this moment ever since the day she accepted the King's contract of marriage, but she was not ready for the Kings embrace until now. She had to follow His instruction and endure His discipline (correction) first, and she admonishes the bride company not to rush others into this place of intimacy before they are ready. The Gazelle is the One who woos and draws the doe there, and the bride company is also not to disturb the couple or disrupt what is taking place.

I Thess. 5:19 Do not quench the Spirit. (NKJV)

Notice here that the Shulamite has matured to a place in the bride company where she is now instructing and admonishing them as well as receiving their ministry to her.

VERSE 8

The Shulamite

The voice of my beloved

Behold, he comes

Leaping upon the mountains,

Skipping upon the hills.

The scene has changed, some time has passed, and now the maiden is in a nice, warm, safe place where she has fallen into a state of complacency and indifference. She is about to experience her second test. There is so much that she must learn before she will be ready to take her place in the Kingdom and move toward her destiny as the King's glorious Bride-Queen.

- *Mountains are symbolic of obstacles.*

- *Hills are symbolic of challenges.*

Both the mountains and the hills have blocked the maiden's view of her Beloved and it is vital for her to keep her focus on him at all times if she is to mature through this time of preparation and run with the King (which means to partner with him in ministry).

Christian, if you have determined to run in this race, you will face these challenges as well. Mountains and hills are things most Christians view as bad and something to be avoided, but notice that the Beloved comes to the maiden upon them. Mountains and hills can be very intimidating, but God, in his great love and infinite wisdom, uses the mountains and the hills in our lives to test us. Tests are needful in order for us to mature to the place where we are able to reach for the Prize and move closer toward our destiny.

Rom. 8:28 And we know that all things work together for good to those who love God, to those who are called according to his purpose. (NKJV)

Much has transpired in the maiden's life between verse 7 where she was enjoying her Beloved's embrace and verse 8. The King had released her and no doubt had called her to run with Him in ministry over the mountains, but the maiden had chosen to remain in the valley of indifference and had allowed the obstacles and challenges in her life to block her view of her Beloved which had resulted in this state of complacency that she now is in.

Do you remember in verse 13 of chapter 1 how the maiden expressed, through her worship, to the King that she was learning to embrace suffering in order to conquer her fear of it? Well, it seems the maiden has gotten stuck in her attempt to conquer that fear – fear of the suffering she most likely would face if she were to follow her Beloved over those hills and mountains, so the King comes to rescue her. At first, she hears his voice.

Rev. 2:7, 11, 17, 29 and Rev. 3:6, 13, and 22 all say, "He who has an ear to hear, let him hear what the Spirit says to the churches." (NKJV)

Matt. 13:9 "He who has ears to hear, let him hear." (NKJV)

John 18:37 "...Everyone who is of the truth hears My voice." (NKJV)

- *Leaping and skipping speak of victoriously overcoming.*

Then she catches sight of Him again. She says, "Look! Here He comes. He has been victorious in overcoming all of the obstacles and challenges that have blocked my view of Him." She must keep her eyes on Him and follow Him over the mountains and hills if she is going to conquer them, for He knows the way. **He is the Way, the Truth, and the Life!**

As we journey through this life, mountains and hills are things we all face and they are mentioned numerous times in the song. They are the very things that the Beloved calls us to climb as you will see in verse 12 of this chapter. He comes to us on the mountains and we must face the mountains with Jesus and conquer them in His power in order to reach our destiny.

Ps. 121:1-2 I will lift up my eyes to the hills – from whence comes my help? My help comes from the Lord who made heaven and earth. (NKJV)

It is the mountains and hills that create the shadow (or fear) when we are in the valley of complacency and indifference. Fear is why so many Christians become stagnant in their walk; some becoming so bound up with it that they are not able to move at all. But our Beloved comes to us like the gazelle, skipping, running, and leaping victoriously over the mountains and He calls us to join Him there for He is ready and able to free us to run with Him.

Ps. 23: 4 Yea, though I walk through the valley of the shadow of death, I will fear no evil, for You are with me... (NKJV)

It is upon these mountains and hills where God dwells. To conquer our fear of them, and to climb their heights running with Jesus over them, is to dwell in His presence.

Christian, what are the mountains and hill in your life? Keep your focus on Jesus, the One who leaps and skips over them. He will show you how to overcome those obstacles and challenges.

Heb. 4:15 For we do not have a High Priest who cannot sympathize with our weaknesses, but was in all points tempted as we are, yet without sin. (NKJV)

VERSE 9

My beloved is like a gazelle or a young stag.

Behold, he stands behind our wall;

He is looking through the windows,

Gazing through the lattice.

- *Gazelle is symbolic of the resurrected Jesus Who overcomes. The gazelle is a fleet-footed animal noted for its attractive eyes and it is native to the Middle East.*

- *Stag speaks of fearlessly conquering all opposition or competition. It is an adult male deer or hart.*

- *Wall is symbolic of one's determination. A wall can keep you safe and protected but it can also become a prison.*

- *Windows speak of looking into the soul through the eyes. It has been said that the eye is the window of the soul.*

- *Matt. 6:22-23 "The lamp of the body is the eye. If therefore your eye is good, your whole body will be full of light. But if your eye is bad, your whole body will be full of darkness. If therefore the light that is in you is darkness, how great is that darkness!" (NKJV)*

- *Lattice speaks of evasiveness.*

The maiden recognizes that her Beloved had conquered all the obstacles in her life. He is fearless in conquering all competition or opposition that might confront her to trip her up, bind her up, or get her off course. He is standing, suggesting that He is ready for action. Yes, He is ready to free her to run.

The maiden refers to the wall as our wall. This is saying that He is determined and ready to support her determination to run with him in ministry. He is looking into her soul and He sees through her evasiveness, her indifference and complacency that are caused by her fear.

The Word has much to say about the Lord's gaze:

> **Jer. 16:17 For my eyes are on all their ways; they are not hidden from My face nor is their iniquity hidden from My eyes. (NKJV)**
>
> **Ps. 39:13 Remove your gaze from me, that I may regain my strength, Before I go away and am no more. (NKJV)**
>
> **Ps. 44:21 Would not God search this out? For He knows the secrets of the heart. (NKJV)**
>
> **Heb. 4:13 And there is no creature hidden from His sight, but all things are naked and open to the eye of Him whom we must give account. (NKJV)**

Christian, when you find yourself in the presence of your Beloved, His gaze will see right through you and if you remain there long enough, His gaze will burn away all the dross in your life until all that is left is pure and holy passion for your King.

VERSE 10

My beloved spoke and said to me:

"Rise up my love, my fair one,

And come away.

Again the King refers to the maiden as His love and He calls her beautiful in her transparent and vulnerable state. He speaks to her so, even though He sees her evasiveness toward Him and He gently woos her.

Prior to this moment, the maiden has spent precious time with the King. She has been under His shade tasting of His fruit and in His banqueting house at His table eating raisin cakes. She has spent time in His embrace, having her mind renewed and her affection captivated. Now He calls her to rise up from the complacency into which she has lapsed, for he is determined and ready for her to run with Him.

Remember how she asked to run with Him earlier in chapter 1? Well, now the maiden, at this point in the song, must be thinking *what? And leave this nice, warm place? Why, there are mountains out there ... I can see the shadows of them across this valley I'm in ... and God only knows what else is out there!!*

She is comfortable and serene just sitting right where she is behind her determination. She is secure and content tucked away from all those problems and challenges out there in the world. She is content to reminisce about her past experience with the King, but He continues to woo her from this place that has now become to her like a prison. Hiding behind her determination to run with Him (words come cheap) has created a prison that holds her back and fear has her bound. This maiden just wants to rest in the King's embrace and feast on the apples and raisin cakes so that she will not have to face the mountains.

VERSE 11

For lo, the winter is past

The rain is over and gone.

- *Winter*

The cold north winds of adversity blow in the winter. The maiden has been in a safe, secure place, protected from it, but sooner or later she must face it and allow the Spirit to use it to do His work in her. She will eventually come to appreciate its purpose in her preparation.

- *Rain*

Water is very scarce in Israel and the rains, early and later, come in the winter. Rain speaks of blessing from God in adversity because the rains were essential to good harvests and plenty. After they had come and gone, then it was time to work and prepare for the harvest.

Solomon says in Ecclesiastes 3:1-2 that there is a season for everything, a time for every purpose under heaven – a time to plant – and it is planting time for them. It is time for this maiden to sow some of that rhema (revelation) Word that she has been feasting on. Read the parable of the sower in Matt. 13:3-4 and 13:18-23.

Timing can be crucial – God's timing, that is. She must learn to obey without hesitation when He calls.

The King continues to woo and draw her just like she asked Him to do in chapter one. He loves her through every stage of this maturing process as He encourages her, challenging her to leave her comfort zone. It is time for her to roll up her sleeves and go to work with Him in His vineyard. Oh, but the maiden wants to stay inside and be fed apples!

Beloved, the Lord calls us to both the drawing aside in intimacy with Him and the running in ministry. We must have a balance of the two! Remember that faith without works is dead.

> **James 2:26 For as the body without the spirit is dead, so**
> **faith without works is dead also. (NKJV)**

VERSE 12

The flowers appear on the earth;

The time of singing has come,

And the voice of the turtledove

Is heard in our land.

- *Flowers are a sign of fruit to come.*

- *Time of singing speaks of harvest time.*

- *Turtledove is a type of the Spirit of God being poured out through the sacrificial work of Jesus.*

It is springtime and flowers always come before the young fruit appears. The Beloved wants her help in His vineyard (His interests) to water and prune the plants in preparation for the coming harvest.

This is evangelism and discipleship and it is an exciting and joyful work that the King wants the maiden to share with Him. The King is saying "Now is the time for salvation." It means sacrificing her own comforts in order to partner with Him in His interests. God pours His Spirit out on this kind of endeavor.

Salvation is being poured out and the Father honors the sacrifice of one's personal interests in order to partner with Jesus and His interests.

VERSE 13

The fig tree puts forth her green figs,

And the vines with the tender grapes

Give a good smell.

Rise up, my love, my fair one,

And come away.

- *Fig tree is symbolic of Israel*

- *The vine is symbolic of the church.*

- *Her green figs speaks of the young, immature nation of Israel.*

When the King speaks of the vineyard, He is speaking of his areas of interest. He is concerned for the welfare of Israel. These are God's chosen people and they need ministry. Genesis 12:3 tells us that God will bless those who bless Israel, and we are commanded to pray for the peace of Jerusalem in Psalm 122:6. Zion is the apple of God's eye as told in Zechariah 2 and, in the context of the Song, Israel is God's wife and the King's mother.

Hosea 2:19-20 I will betroth you to Me forever
Yes, I will betroth you to me
In righteousness and justice.

In loving kindness and mercy.
I will betroth you to Me in faithfulness,
And you shall know the Lord. (NKJV)

In Luke 19:41-44 Jesus wept over Jerusalem because she did not know the time of her visitation. Jerusalem speaks of the mature bride of Christ in the Kingdom of Heaven, made up of Jew and Gentile as referred to in Revelation 21:9-27. The King is also concerned for His church. He is after a bride-queen and He wants her at His side in the Kingdom. I believe this is why God ensured that this Song was not excluded from the Bible for it contains this vital message to the church. It shows you and me how to gain the Prize.

Is it any wonder, in the light of these scriptures, that Israel is very special to our Lord, and we, the church, have been grafted into her? Jew and Gentile, one in the spirit, is referred to as the olive tree and it is talked about in Romans 9, 10, and 11. We will see in the sixth chapter of the song the prophetic fulfillment of this which is God's plan for His people. Oh, how Satan, the one who divides with no cause, has worked to prevent this from coming to pass down through the ages.

- *Tender grapes are new converts in the church.*

Also mentioned here is the fruit of the vine who are young Christians (the tender grapes) in the church who must be discipled. The King says that there is evidence that they are ready.

The King asks her a second time to rise up out of her complacency, her lack of trust or whatever it is that is holding her back and come away with Him. He is asking her to run in ministry with Him for there is much work to be done in his vineyard (His interests). The olive tree (Jew and Gentile, one in the spirit), or Israel and the church, must be pruned and watered (discipled) so that they will produce the abundant fruit that God desires.

Notice here that the King reemphasizes His love for the maiden and proclaims her beauty once again, even in this state of indecision and evasiveness concerning His interests.

VERSE 14

Oh, my dove, in the clefts of the rock

In the secret places of the cliff,

Let me see your face.

Let me hear your voice;

For your voice is sweet,

And your face is lovely.

The King knows that the maiden is going to compromise, but He still calls her "My dove" (the one who is focused on Him alone). He is seeing in her the finished work and He calls her to the clefts of the rock in the secret places of the cliffs. The clefts and the cliffs are on the mountains and hills.

The King calls the maiden fair in verse 10. She is available to Him for intimacy, but He wants to have intimate fellowship with her as they run in ministry and she is hesitant to run because of her fear of the mountains.

Saints of God, there is a secret place where we can enjoy intimate time alone with Jesus, while climbing the mountains and hills together. Spending intimate time with our Beloved in the secret place is absolutely essential to us if we are going to conquer those obstacles that challenge us in this life.

The King is calling the maiden to run with Him over the mountains and hills. She must face them, but she must face them with her eyes on Him.

> **Ps. 121:1-8 I will lift up my eyes to the hills-**
> **From whence comes my help?**
> **My help comes from the Lord,**
> **Who made Heaven and earth.**
> **He will not allow your foot to be moved;**
> **He who keeps you will not slumber.**
> **Behold, He who keeps Israel**
> **Shall not slumber nor sleep.**
> **The Lord is your keeper;**
> **The Lord is your shade at your right hand.**
> **The sun shall not strike you by day,**
> **Nor the moon by night.**
> **The Lord shall preserve you from all evil;**
> **He shall preserve your soul.**
> **The Lord shall preserve your going out and your coming in**
> **From this time forth and even forevermore. (NKJV)**

The King is asking the maiden to lift her eyes to Him, to rise up, overcome her fears and face the mountains of obstacles. Her obedience to do this makes her lovely in His sight. He wants to hear her voice as she lifts it in prayer. He wants to hear her confessions of faith and her testimony, for her voice is sweet to His ear and these things will help her to overcome the hills and mountains that she is facing.

Christian, the Bridegroom, Jesus, calls to you today to the clefts and cliffs on the mountains. He wants to see your eyes focused on Him as you face the mountains and hills in your life. He longs to hear your voice lifted to Him in prayer and in your confessions of faith. He longs to hear your testimony, the testimony of an overcomer!

VERSE 15

HER BROTHERS

Catch us the foxes,

The little foxes that spoil the vines,

For our vines have tender grapes

- *Foxes are sources of vexation.*

- *Little foxes are small, irritating vexations.*

- *Vines speak of the church.*

- *Tender grapes are the new Christians in the church.*

Remember the maiden's brothers? Well, here they are again, those religious, legalistic, controlling individuals in the church. These folks get really nervous when others in the church get a little too intimate with the Lord or too spiritual, because then, they are not able to control them.

They are thinking that their sister has just "gone off the deep end," so the brothers, in an attempt to manipulate her, very slyly ask her to take care of these small, irritating church matters. They know these matters are not her area of responsibility but theirs. They want her under their thumb and use these tactics which have worked before.

The maiden succumbs to their tactics at first because she loves and cares about her church family very much. But then...

VERSE 16

THE SHULAMITE

My beloved is mine and I am his.

He feeds his flock among the lilies.

The maiden recognizes that she is being drawn off course and she gets refocused. She is saying, "Hey, wait a minute! I belong to my Beloved and He is feeding His followers among the lilies (The bride company who have determined to be His Bride-Queen) and that is where I need to be! Chasing foxes for my brothers is not what I'm supposed to be doing!"

VERSE 17

(TO HER BELOVED)

Until the day breaks

And the shadows flee away,

Turn, my beloved,

And be like a gazelle

Or a young stag

Upon the mountains of Bether.

- *Shadows are symbolic of fear.*

- *Bether means separation.*

The maiden realizes too late that she has been influenced by the manipulation and control of her brothers and her fear of their displeasure. She sees that her Beloved is gone and she calls to Him to turn around and come back to her until this dark time passes. She has waited too long to obey His voice and she has allowed this mountain to separate them so that she can no longer see Him in His resurrection power as He fearlessly conquers all opposition to her.

Our Shulamite has failed her second test! As a result, this maiden is suffering through a hard time once again. She is experiencing the discipline of separation now.

This is when the Lord removes His manifested presence from our lives in order to draw us after Him. Jesus has promised in Hebrews 13:5 that He will never leave nor forsake us, but we need to understand that there is a difference in His presence with us and His **manifested** presence.

Let me give you an example. Let's imagine that you took your child with you to the local mall. You had taken great pains to instruct her to stay with you, and you told her of the dangers of wandering off. Suppose that your child had forgotten your conversation and wandered off in spite of your careful instruction, but you had kept her in your sight. You hide behind a counter and watch as that child suddenly realizes that you are not to be seen anywhere and she is lost, alone, and frightened. She begins to frantically search for you. Now, you would never leave that child alone and unattended, but you would remain out of her sight just long enough to teach her a lesson. In this circumstance, you would teach her a valuable lesson that might save her from a potentially dangerous situation later on.

The maiden is in a potentially harmful state and the King is drawing her after Him and out of this place of complacency by removing His manifested presence from her. She must reposition herself to be able to focus on Him again so that she can see to follow and run with Him in ministry.

The King loves her too much to let her stagnate in her walk and let her settle for less than what she has determined to gain: **the goal of the Prize of the upward call of God in Christ Jesus.**

Have you experienced in your spiritual journey a time such as this? We call it a "dry" time.

Can you pinpoint what may have caused the Lord to remove his manifested presence for a season?

Did it make you thirsty enough to rise up out of your circumstances to pursue Him?

CHAPTER TWO REVIEW

1. Which two flowers does the Shulamite compare herself to? _____

_____

2. Why does the Beloved compare the maiden to a lily among thorns? _____

_____

3. Why does the maiden compare her Beloved to an apple tree? _____

_____

4. Who are the enemies of the Shulamite and whom do they represent today? _____

_____

5. When the Beloved embraces the maiden, His two actions represent what? _____

_____

6. Mountains and hills are symbolic of what? _____

_____

7. Leaping and skipping are symbols of what? _____

_____

8. New converts are described as what? _____

_____

9. Why do the maiden's brothers ask her to catch the little foxes? _____

_____

10. Fear is symbolized by what? _____

_____

CHAPTER THREE

THE PALANQUIN

VERSE 1

THE SHULAMITE

By night on my bed I sought the one I love;

I sought him but I did not find him.

- *Night speaks of a dark, hard time and suffering.*

The maiden is once again suffering through another dark, hard time in her life. She is going through a spiritually dry and lonely time, separated from the manifested presence of her beloved King.

In chapter 1, she was enjoying His rest, referred to as **our bed.** She had submitted to His will and had ceased to strive in her flesh against His will and it was a pleasant and productive time in her life.

Now her rest is referred to here as **my bed**, which is complacent, evasive, and compromising behavior regarding the King's interests. It has only produced unfruitful, restlessness in her life. Unfruitfulness is a dangerous state to be in!

> **Matt. 3:8, 10 "Therefore bear fruits worthy of repentance ... every tree which does not bear good fruit is cut down and thrown into the fire. (NKJV)**

The King loves this maiden too much to allow her to remain in this dangerous state. He revealed Himself to her and called her to run. When she did not respond, He removed His manifested presence from her, knowing she would rise up out of the state she was in and seek after Him.

VERSE 2

"I will rise now," I said,

"And go about the city;

In the streets and in the squares

I will seek the one I love."

I sought him, but I did not find him.

- *City is symbolic of worldliness.*

The Shulamite had been held in the King's embrace in the previous chapter. It was a wonderful time of intimacy with Him, but after the King had released her and left that place of intimacy, she evidently allowed the brothers to distract her focus away from her Beloved and she became quite comfortable and satisfied to remain in her complacency. She was reluctant to follow her Beloved even when He returned to her and called her repeatedly to come away and run with Him in ministry.

Now she rises up from what has become her spiritually dark, stagnant condition and she goes out into the worldly, materialistic city looking for Him.

It has been my experience that we do not remain stationary very long in our walk with the Lord. If we are not progressing with Him, then we are digressing from Him. This is the case with the maiden in this verse. The Beloved remains hidden from her for she does not find Him in the busy, going to and fro, social life of the city.

His instruction to her in chapter 1, verse 8 was to embrace the body of Christ within her mother's house and serve there under their training and covering where she was nurtured in the things of God and where she would mature in servitude.

Christian, let me encourage you, if you have experienced a hurtful situation within your church family, isolating yourself, as the maiden has done here in order to avoid those unpleasant brothers, will not solve anything. You certainly will not find your answers out in the world! Most likely you will encounter the same challenges where ever you go until you finally face them and depend on the Lord to help you grow through them. Let me encourage you, idle complacency will not help you gain the Prize.

VERSE 3

The watchmen who go about the city found me;

I said, "Have you seen the one I love?"

- ***Watchmen are God appointed leaders who watch over the church worldwide and they point all to Jesus.***

Watchmen may serve in the office of prophet, apostle, intercessor, etc. These leaders are firmly planted in the life of the church but the majority of their ministry takes place outside the church. These discerning watchmen see the struggling maiden wandering the streets of the city and when she inquires about direction from them, they point her to her Beloved.

VERSE 4

Scarcely had I passed by them,

When I found the one I love.

I held him and would not let him go,

Until I had brought him to the house of my mother,

And into the chamber of her who conceived me.

The maiden followed the directions of the watchmen, for she finds her Beloved and holds Him close to her, not intending to ever let Him go out of her sight again.

Jesus promises that all who seek shall find!

> **Matt. 7:7 "Ask, and it will be given to you; seek, and you will find; knock, and it will be opened to you." (NKJV)**

> **Is. 55:6 Seek the Lord while He may be found, Call upon Him while He is near. (NKJV)**

One tends to appreciate, more than ever before, those precious things that they once thought were lost to them. The maiden has discovered a new, holy embrace that is a result of her season of spiritual struggle and she will not let Him go this time! She does not want to risk ever losing His manifested presence again.

- *Her mother symbolizes the church. It is the place where she was introduced to the things of God.*

The maiden carries her Beloved into the house of her mother. She wants all in her church family to have an intimate, passionate, life-changing relationship with the King like the one she is enjoying.

She even carries Him into the inner workings of the church. Sometimes the leadership within our churches becomes so inundated with church matters that they need to be reminded to spend intimate time with the Lord to be refreshed and renewed. It is the balance of the running and the drawing that this maiden is learning and she wants to share it with her church family.

Jesus draws us today and we hold Him in intimacy. We carry Him in the witness of our lives and in our testimony. We carry Him into the church where we attend to encourage and build up our church family – this is **discipleship.** Then we run with Him to partner with Him in His work out in the fields – this is **evangelism.** Jesus calls us all to be involved in both the drawing and the running as He directs.

VERSE 5

I charge you, O daughters of Jerusalem,

By the gazelles, or by the does of the field,

Do not stir up nor awaken love

Until it pleases.

This is the second embrace in the song. The first embrace was in chapter 2, verse 7. In the first embrace, the Beloved carried the Shulamite into the banqueting house where He embraced her. This time the Shulamite maiden is carrying her Beloved as she goes back into her church and she is holding Him. She has initiated this embrace.

Again she admonishes the daughters of Jerusalem not to disturb the couple or what is taking place here. Neither are they to rush others into this place of intimacy prematurely.

We are admonished in 1 Thessalonians 5:19 *not to quench the Spirit.* Ephesians 4:30 tells us *not to grieve the Holy Spirit* and Hebrews 10:29 instructs us *not to insult the Spirit.* How many times do well-meaning people, who are insensitive to the moving of the Holy Spirit in another's life, get in the way and disrupt the work that the Spirit is needing to do there? We will see, in the next verse, that while the maiden is embracing her Beloved, she sees spiritual truths in a vision that will help to prepare her for her journey through the wilderness.

What lessons did the Shulamite learn from this test?

1. The instant she hears her Beloved say, "Rise up ... and come away!", she must obey, without hesitation and in total trust.

2. She must listen to and obey His voice alone. She is not to serve the interests of others, but she is to serve His interests alone – even when the interests of others seem to be worthwhile. She must keep her eyes on her Beloved at all times.

3. She cannot put her Beloved in a box. Jesus comes for all in the world who are lost. He belongs to the nations. We cannot hold Him selfishly to our lives alone. No, we've agreed to partner with Him to go into all the world with Him, so that all may have the opportunity to know Him as we do. She cannot erect a memorial and get comfortably complacent in the memory of that place to which He brought her and in which He blessed her.

Beloved, we must keep our eyes on Jesus and follow Him. He doesn't stay still long and if we stop, He continues to move. We are then in danger of getting stagnant in our spiritual walk. If you are in that state right now, then let me encourage you to seek Him with all your heart. Please do not stop short of the Prize!

VERSE 6

FRIENDS AND RELATIVES

Who is this coming out of the wilderness

Like pillars of smoke,

Perfumed with myrrh and frankincense,

With all the merchant's fragrant powders?

- *Wilderness is the place of no other provision but God's and it is symbolic of our wandering through this world.*

There are mountains and hills in the wilderness to be conquered as we journey through it in this life!

- *Pillars of smoke is God's manifested presence.*

- *Perfumed (fragrant) is the evidence of:*

- *Myrrh is symbolic of suffering love.*

- *Frankincense is symbolic of intercession.*

- *Merchant's fragrant powders speaks of the evidences of total surrender to God.*

- *Friends and relatives are the wedding guests in this scene of the song.*

The scene has changed. In the previous verse, the maiden was embracing the King. In this verse, we see friends and relatives observing an entourage coming out of the wilderness. (Some NKJV translations attribute this verse to the Shulamite, herself, while others have portrayed it as the wedding party made up of friends of Solomon). I believe this scene in the song is describing a vision that the maiden sees while in the King's presence. The next 16 verses describe this vision.

There is a wedding about to take place. It is the wedding festivities for the King and the Shulamite maiden. The wedding guests are waiting for their arrival and they see this entourage coming out of the wilderness.

Who is it? It is Solomon and his friends, and it is the Shulamite maiden being carried inside Solomon's couch upon their shoulders. They have been in God's manifested presence as they have wandered in the wilderness, and God alone has provided their every need. Together they have conquered all the mountains and hills of the wilderness and there is evidence that they have been seasoned in suffering love and intercession. They are totally surrendered to God! Together they have overcome the world and its influence on the maiden's life.

Rom. 12:2 And do not be conformed to this world, but be transformed by the renewing of your mind, that you may prove what is that good and acceptable and perfect will of God. (NKJV)

I John 2:15 Do not love the world or the things of the world. If anyone loves the world, the love of the Father is not in him. (NKJV)

I John 5:4-5 For whatever is born of God overcomes the world. And this is the victory that has overcome the world – our faith. Who is he who overcomes the world, but he who believes that Jesus is the Son of God? (NKJV)

I John 5:19 We know that we are of God, and the whole world lies under the sway of the wicked one. (NKJV)

VERSE 7

Behold it is Solomon's couch,

With sixty valiant men around it,

Of the valiant men of Israel.

- *Valiant men are the brave warriors of God who have served Him in the body of Christ.*

- *The valiant of Israel are the courageous warriors of God who have served Him and His people down through the ages.*

- *Solomon's couch – this couch is symbolic of our faith in God and His word, and the gospel message of Jesus Christ.*

The couch was a mobile carriage in which one could rest safely as it was carried on the strong shoulders of one's servants from one place to another.

I believe that this couch is symbolic of our faith in God's Son, Jesus, and His completed work on the cross. I believe that it carries us through the wilderness and through the mountains and hills of problems and challenges that we face on our life's journey right into the manifested presence of God.

This couch is surrounded and carried by 60 brave servants, warriors of God who serve in the body of Christ and who have served God down through the ages. These people are true servants of the Most High God and heroes of the faith.

> **Heb. 12:1-2 Therefore we also, since we are surrounded by so great a cloud of witnesses, let lay aside every weight, and the sin which so easily ensnares us, and let us run with endurance the race that is set before us, looking unto Jesus, the author and finisher of our faith, who for the joy was set before Him endured the cross... (NKJV)**

In ancient Jewish tradition, the bridegroom and his friends would surprise the bride with a sudden shout and then whisk her away from her bedchamber into the night. She was carried safely through the streets of the city to her wedding day in a couch or palanquin by the friends of the bridegroom. The bride and groom, upon their arrival at the home of the groom's father, would go into the bridal chamber and the friend of the bridegroom would wait outside at the door listening for the voice of the bridegroom to confirm that the marriage had been consummated.

In John 3:28-29, we find these words spoken by John the Baptist, "You yourselves bear me witness, that I said "I am not the Christ," but, "I have been sent before Him." "He who has the bride is the bridegroom, but the friends of the bridegroom, who stands and hears him, rejoices greatly because of the bridegroom's voice. Therefore this joy of mine is fulfilled."

I believe that John the Baptist is just one example of the many brave and courageous men and women that make up this group mentioned here.

There are 60 valiant men.

In scripture:

10 is the fullness of testing.
6 is the number of man.
60 would be the fullness of man's testing.

These valiant men have endured the fullness of man's testing.

James 1:2-3 My brothers, count it all joy when you fall into various trials, knowing that the testing of your faith produces endurance. (NKJV)

These people have stood strong in their faith down through the ages and they stand with the maiden in her faith.

VERSE 8

They all hold swords,

Being experts in war

Every man has his sword on his thigh

Because of fear in the night.

- *Sword speaks of the Word of God*

Heb. 4:12 For the Word of God is living and powerful and sharper than any two-edged sword.

- *Thigh speaks of strength.*

- *War speaks of spiritual warfare.*

- *Night is referring to dark, hard times and suffering.*

These men are trained and strong in the Word. They are ready for warfare. They are ready to come against the fear that would torment the maiden during those dark, hard times in her life.

Note that it is fear which the valiant men come against. The enemy has already been defeated. Fear of the hard times, as we go through the wilderness, is the real culprit in our lives. Many times it is this fear that paralyzes us in our journey.

VERSE 9

Of the wood of Lebanon,

Solomon the King

Made himself a palanquin:

- *Wood symbolizes Jesus' humanity.*

- *Lebanon symbolizes God's glory and majesty.*

- *Palanquin is a traveling couch.*

The King made this traveling couch when He left God's glory and majesty to take on humanity in order to rescue His bride and bring her to her place in God's Kingdom.

Psalm 91 is a beautiful picture of the palanquin! Our faith in God and the gospel of Jesus Christ our Savior is what carries us safely through life's journey to our final destiny.

VERSE 10

He made its pillars of silver,

Its supports of gold,

Its seat of purple

Its interior paved with love

By the daughters of Jerusalem.

- *Pillars symbolize the overcomer.*

- *Silver symbolizes redemption.*

- *Support is the foundation.*

- *Gold is symbolic of God's divine nature.*

- *Seat speaks of rest from labor.*

- *Purple is symbolic of royalty and kingly authority.*

This is saying to me that an "overcoming power" comes from our redemption. Because we now belong to Jesus, this power comes from Him by faith in His completed work on the cross. The support of gold says to me that God's divine nature – His unconditional love for mankind – is the whole reason for faith. Faith is to carry us into His arms; to have our fellowship with Him restored back to the way it was in the very beginning, before sin, when Adam and Eve walked with him in the garden.

The remarks about the interior of the palanquin say to me that the couch is enclosed or embraced by the love of the Shulamite's support group, the daughters of Jerusalem, and their willingness to give into the interests of the King.

Their love embraces her as she is being transformed and refined. The palanquin carries her through the hard, dry places of the wilderness as her faith is being tested.

I John 3:16 By this we know love, because He laid down His life for us. And we also ought to lay down our lives for the brethren. (NKJV)

John 13:35 "By this all will know that you are My disciples if you have love for one another." (NKJV)

The purple seat says to me that there is a rest from our own labors to be enjoyed as we follow our Beloved and submit to His Kingly authority over us. We can trust Him. Our faith in His completed work on the cross will carry us safely through the wilderness into God's presence and to our destiny.

... see King Solomon with the crown with which His mother crowned Him on the day of His wedding, the day of the gladness of His heart.

Song of Solomon 3:11

KS '06'

VERSE 11

Go forth, O daughters of Zion,

And see King Solomon with the crown

With which his mother crowned him

On the day of his wedding,

The day of the gladness in his heart.

The daughters of Zion are those who have become the mature bride down through the ages. They have reached the goal of the Prize of the upward call of God in Christ Jesus.

> **Heb. 12:22-24 But you have come to Mount Zion and to the city of the living God, the heavenly Jerusalem, to an innumerable company of angels who are registered in heaven, to God the Judge of all, to the spirits of just men made perfect, to Jesus the Mediator of the new covenant... (NKJV)**

The crown is the King's mature bride, prepared and ready to take her place at His side in the Kingdom as His queen. The work of the Holy Spirit has been completed in her, she has endured the fullness of testing and she is ready to join the ranks of the daughters of Zion. She is His reward!

> **Prov. 12:4 An excellent wife is the crown of her husband.**

> **Is. 62:1-7 For Zion's sake I will not hold My peace,**
> **And for Jerusalem's sake I will not rest,**
> **Until her righteousness goes forth as brightness,**
> **And her salvation as a lamp that burns.**
> **The Gentiles shall see your righteousness,**
> **And all kings your glory.**
> **You shall be called by a new name,**
> **Which the mouth of the Lord will name.**
> **You shall also be a crown of glory**
> **In the hand of the Lord,**
> **And a royal diadem**
> **In the hand of your God.**
> **You shall no longer be termed**
> **Forsaken,**
> **Nor shall your land any more be termed Desolate;**
> **But you shall be called Hephzibah**
> **and your land, Beulah;**
> **For the Lord delights in you,**

And your land shall be married.
For as a young man marries a virgin,
So shall your sons marry you,
And as the bridegroom rejoices over the bride,
So shall your God rejoice over you.
I have set watchmen on your wall,
O Jerusalem,
They shall never hold their peace day or night.
You who make mention of the Lord, do not keep silent,
And give Him no rest till He establishes
And till He makes Jerusalem a praise in the earth. (NKJV)

Zeph 3:17 ...He will quiet you with His love,
He will rejoice over you with singing. (NKJV)

The beloved Bridegroom King rejoices over His bride on this day – the day of the gladness of His heart! He is singing over the maiden.

- *His mother would be Israel, for Israel is referred to in Hosea as God's wife.*

Hos. 2:19-20 I will betroth you to Me forever,
Yes, I will betroth you to Me
In righteousness and justice,
In lovingkindness and mercy;
I will betroth you to Me in faithfulness,
And you shall know the Lord. (NKJV)

The wedding guests are still speaking and they are calling forth the mature bride company to come and see this Shulamite maiden on her wedding day as she is presented to her Beloved King by His mother, Israel.

This is a prophetic picture of Israel's acceptance, not only of the Messiah, Jesus, but of His bride as well, as spoken of in Ephesians 2:14-16, which is made of Jew and Gentile. It is also a prophetic picture of Israel's return to God from her harlotries. Israel, the King's mother and God's wife, will set the bride in place as she places the crown upon the King's head. There at His side, she will rule and reign with Him in God's Kingdom.

The palanquin carries the Shulamite maiden to her wedding day, the day of the gladness of the King's heart. They will enter what I believe to be the bridal chamber that He has prepared for her. This is another of the secret places where private intimacy with the King is shared. There are no hidden secrets between them in this place.

Ps. 44:21 Would not God search this out?
For he knows the secret of the heart. (NKJV)

Child of God, He knows the secrets of your heart, but you need to know that He knows!

Heb. 4:13 And there is no creature that is hidden from His sight, but all things are naked and open to the eyes of Him to whom we must give account. (NKJV)

II Cor. 3:18 But we all, with unveiled face, beholding as in a mirror the glory of the Lord, are being transformed into the same image from glory to glory just as by the Spirit of the Lord. (NKJV)

Here in this vision of the bridal chamber, the maiden is totally and completely transparent before the King's scrutiny as she gazes into his face. The dramatic transformation in the maiden, due to the refining process that has taken place in her life, has produced a glorious bride fit for the King who is ready to fulfill her destiny.

Mal. 3:3 He will sit as a refiner and a purifier of silver; He will purify the sons of Levi and purge them as gold and silver. (NKJV)

And the two will become one there in the bridal chamber.

Eph. 5:30-32 For we are members of His body, of His flesh and of His bones. For this reason a man shall leave his father and mother and be joined to his wife, and the two shall become one flesh. This is a great mystery but I speak concerning Christ and the church. (NKJV)

I Cor. 6:17-20 But he who is joined to the Lord is one spirit with Him. For you were bought at a price; therefore glorify God in your body and in your spirit, which are God's. (NKJV)

CHAPTER THREE REVIEW

1. What caused the King to remove His manifested presence from the Shulamite? _____

_____

2. The God-appointed leaders who watch over the church and point all to Jesus are called

_____

3. These leaders could be serving as _____

_____

4. When the maiden finds her Beloved, where does she take Him and what does that place represent?

_____

5. Solomon's couch (the palanquin) is symbolic of what? _____

_____

6. The 60 valiant men represent what? _____

_____

7. The sword represents what? _____

_____

8. Who are the daughters of Zion? _____

_____

9. The palanquin is made of the wood of Lebanon. Wood and Lebanon represent what?

_____

10. The palanquin's supports of gold represent what? _____

_____

CHAPTER FOUR

THE WEDDING

VERSE 1

THE BELOVED

Behold, you are fair, my love!

Behold, you are fair!

You have dove's eyes behind your veil.

Your hair is like a flock of goats,

Going down from Mount Gilead.

- *Fair means unveiled, beautiful, or transparent.*

- *Doves' eyes are focused on only one thing at a time.*

The dove is also symbolic of the Holy Spirit in scripture.

> **Matt. 3:16b ... and He saw the Spirit of God descending like a dove and alighting upon Him.**

The maiden's ability to focus on her Beloved alone is a characteristic of the Holy Spirit's effect upon her life.

> **John 14:26 "But the helper, the Holy Spirit, whom the Father will send in My name, He will teach you all things, and bring to your remembrance all things that I said to you." (NKJV)**

> **John 15:26 "But when the Helper comes, whom I shall send to you from the Father, the Spirit of truth who proceeds from the Father, He will testify of Me." (NKJV)**

> **John 16:13-14 "However, when He, the Spirit of truth, has come, He will guide you into all truth, for He will not speak on His own authority, by whatever He hears He will speak; and He will tell you things to come. He will glorify Me, for He will take of what is Mine and declare it to you." (NKJV)**

- *Veil is symbolic of her servitude in and through the body of Christ within the church and it says to the world that she belongs to her Beloved.*

- *Hair is symbolic of separation unto God.*

- *Flock of goats is referring to those the maiden is responsible to God to care for and disciple.*

- *Going down speaks of humbling oneself.*

The King admires the maiden's willingness to reach out and minister to the needs of the lost and to those less fortunate.

The couple is alone in what, I believe, is the bridal chamber and the King removes the maiden's veil and begins to affirm her beauty. When the Lord repeats something, He is wanting to emphasize what He is saying to the listener. It is important to the King that the maiden knows that she is beautiful to Him! While the maiden is still and quiet before the King, He begins to minister to the deepest part of her – that part that no one else has seen. The maiden is encouraged by the prophetic words of the King in her vision. He describes the finished work which He sees the Holy Spirit doing in her. It is a work that will be perfected through the fullness of testing.

> **Phil. 1:6 ...being confident of this very thing, that He who has begun a good work in you will complete it until the day of Jesus Christ. (NKJV)**

Saints of God, do you realize that what we are given here and in the next four verses is a vivid picture – a detailed description of the glorious bride of Christ on her wedding day? This is a mirror for us to look upon so that we can know how we are supposed to be, as His spotless bride, when He returns for us.

> **I Cor. 13:12 now we see but a poor reflection as in a mirror, then we shall see face to face. Now I know in part, then I shall know fully, even as I am fully known. (NIV)**

The prophet, Hosea, tells us that we are destroyed from a lack of knowledge and Solomon tells us in the Proverbs that we perish for a lack of vision.

Well, dear ones, here we have a vision to move toward. In this song we are given the knowledge we need that will enable us to fulfill our destiny in God's kingdom, provided that we will seek God for understanding.

The King is voicing His admiration of the virtues He sees in the maiden in a very intimate way. Not used until now, He is using language only a husband would use after the union has been consummated. The couple has become one and the maiden's interests and the King's interests are becoming one and the same.

The maiden will begin to learn about the King's interests. She will learn about those things that are important to Him – things which are essential for her to know before she can take her place beside Him in the Kingdom.

Dr. David Jeremiah said the following words in his radio broadcast when speaking about marriage, "...there is a constant unveiling that takes place in a marriage relationship that keeps one transparent before another and therefore vulnerable to one another." This is a true statement and it is also true here in this relationship between the King and the maiden of the Song.

In the vision the King sees and admires this maiden's ability to stay focused on Him as she stands before Him unveiled, transparent, vulnerable, and available. This is a time of self examination for the maiden as she sees this vision while in the King's embrace.

I Cor. 11:28a But let a man examine himself... (NKJV)

Gal. 6:4 But let each one examine his own work, and then he will have rejoicing in himself alone, and not in another. (NKJV)

Beloved, it is important for us to examine ourselves and our work as the Lord requires, and do this in His presence – alone with Him. Jesus is the One we must be concerned about pleasing. He is our example and the One to follow and pattern our lives after.

In the vision the King affirms this maiden's separation unto God and her commitment to Him to care for the flock of goats that she has been given.

Mount Gilead was a fertile area where goats fed on abundant food. The King takes note of the fact that she is diligent to serve her flock well.

VERSE 2

Your teeth are like a flock of shorn sheep

Which have come up from the washing,

Every one of which bears twins,

And none is barren among them.

- *Teeth are symbolic of the ability to chew and digest the meat of the Word and not just the milk of the Word which is for baby Christians (those who have recently accepted Christ).*

I Cor. 3:1-2 And I, brethren, could not speak to you as to spiritual people but as to carnal, as to babes in Christ. I fed you with milk and not with solid food; for until now you were not able to receive it, and even now you are still not able. (NKJV)

- *"Shorn sheep which have come up from the washing" is speaking of those who are in Jesus' flock (those who serve as they follow Him) who have been washed in His word.*

These sheep are shorn – they serve! They give of themselves for others in their servitude. They have come up – they have been promoted! They are washed – they are transformed! The darkness from the effects of sin on their lives is no longer there.

- ***Twins speak of balance.***

These sheep produce more sheep that are balanced in the Word!

- ***Barren speaks of unfruitfulness.***

These sheep are fruitful and productive.

The King is saying that the maiden is able to rightly handle the Word of Truth. She has learned and matured under the authority and teaching of the body of Christ, His flock.

> **II Tim. 2:15 Be diligent to present yourself approved to God, a worker who does not need to be ashamed, rightly dividing the word of truth. (NKJV)**

The King is saying that the maiden has been promoted in her servitude and that she has been washed in a balance of the Word. He sees that her life is producing fruit and is also producing fruit in the lives of others.

Notice in the previous verse, that the maiden's flock is referred to as goats, implying willful, stubborn disobedience. In this verse, however, they are spoken of as sheep. Sheep know their shepherd's voice and they follow him. This transformation comes about in the maiden's flock as she diligently serves them and feeds them a balance of the Word. They have learned from her example and have followed her instruction and now they are able to reproduce and have themselves become fruitful in the Kingdom. This is a pattern, and it is God's plan to evangelize the world so that all who will, can know Him, find their place in the Kingdom, and live eternally in His presence, enjoying the abundant life that He offers to all.

VERSE 3

Your lips are like a strand of scarlet,

And your mouth is lovely.

Your temples behind your veil

Are like a piece of pomegranate.

- ***Lips are symbolic of receiving His kisses (instruction and discipline) in ministry.***

- ***Strand of scarlet speaks of salvation through the blood of Jesus.***

- *Mouth is symbolic of speaking the Word; speech.*

- *Temples refer to one's thought life.*

- *Pomegranate is symbolic of the priesthood.*

The King is admiring the words of the maiden in the vision. She is speaking the Word in which He has instructed her. She is an evangelist that preaches salvation through the blood of Jesus. The fact that she spends intimate time with Him receiving His kisses (which are His instructions and His discipline) makes her lovely to Him. She is transparent under His scrutiny in the bridal chamber and He says her thought life is pure. She shows others that she belongs to Him through her servitude in the body of Christ. (You will remember that in the King's embrace, His left hand is under her head, renewing her mind). This maiden is first called to the priesthood of God in this vision of the bridal chamber. We will see her fulfill this call as she moves toward a dramatic climax in chapter 7 of this Song.

(An interesting side note is that a pomegranate acts as an antioxidant in the human body. It arrests free radicals which destroy healthy cells.)

We are instructed in Philippians 4:8 to think and meditate on the things that are true, noble, just, lovely, of good report, and those things that are virtuous and praiseworthy. II Corinthians 10:5 encourages us to bring every thought into captivity to the obedience of Christ, much like the pomegranate arrests harmful free radicals in the human body. Matthew 9:4 tells us that Jesus knows our thoughts.

A pure, Godly thought life is a prerequisite to the priesthood.

A priest is a go-between for God and man, until that man is reconciled to God. In the priesthood, every area of that priest's life is dictated to and absorbed in God's purposes. A priest is called holy unto God. A priest's habitat is God's presence.

Pomegranates were used as an ornament on the robes of the Levitical high priest of Israel in the Old Testament. Jesus is a priest that intercedes on our behalf before God.

Saints of God, in like manner, we are a royal priesthood and our habitat is God's presence. We were created to function properly in that atmosphere, and that is why we malfunction when we are outside that atmosphere.

I Pet. 2:9 But you are a chosen generation, a royal priesthood, a holy nation, His own special people that you may proclaim the praises of Him who called you out of darkness into His marvelous light; (NKJV)

When we read about Israel in the Old Testament, we see that the priesthood has always been extremely important to God and it continues to be one of His primary interests, as we will see when we read further into the Song.

VERSE 4

Your neck is like the tower of David,

Built for an armory,

On which hang a thousand bucklers,

All shields of mighty men.

- *Neck is symbolic of one's will.*
- *Tower speaks of being alert to the plans of the enemy.*

- *Armory speaks of preparedness for battle.*

- *Thousand speaks of fullness; a full number.*

- *Mighty men speaks of spiritual warriors.*

The King sees that the maiden has set her will to be spiritually alert to the plans of the enemy at all times. She is prepared and ready at a moment's notice for spiritual warfare. She is participating with and supportive of all (a full number) spiritual warriors (like the valiant men who carried her to her wedding day mentioned in chapter 3, verses 7 and 8)

Rest assured, Christian, that we will see the maiden become the spiritual warrior, over whom the King is prophetically proclaiming in this vision before the Song ends.

VERSE 5

Your two breasts are like two fawns,

Twins of a gazelle,

Which feed among the lilies.

- *Two speaks of the two testaments.*

- *Twins symbolize balance.*

- *Breasts are symbolic of the ability to nurture others.*

- *Fawns speaks of the young who stay near their mother, the doe mentioned in chapter 3, verse5.*

- *Gazelle is symbolic of the resurrected Jesus.*

- *Lilies are symbolic of the Bride-Queen.*

The King sees the Shulamite maiden as able to nurture the church with a balanced teaching from the Old Testament as well as from the New Testament of the resurrected Jesus. He sees her nurturing those who have just entered the ranks of the bride company. He is describing His glorious Bride-Queen in this vision – a Bride-Queen who is prepared and ready to take her place in the Kingdom as she instructs others to do likewise.

VERSE 6

Until the day breaks

And the shadows flee away,

I will go my way to the mountain of myrrh

And the hill of frankincense.

- *Myrrh symbolizes suffering love.*

- *Frankincense symbolizes intercession.*

The King must foresee another dark, fearful time of testing for the maiden, because He is telling her that He must leave her embrace and the comforts that it affords, and go into a time of intercession for her. Yes, what the King has just prophetically proclaimed over the maiden in the vision only comes through the fullness of testing. We see the King demonstrating "suffering love" at this point in the verse, for he is willing to leave the comforts of their intimate time together to go into a time of intercession for her.

> **Heb. 7:25 Therefore He is also able to save to the uttermost those who come to God through Him, since He always lives to make intercession for them. (NKJV)**

Beloved, there will be times as a part of the royal priesthood when the Lord will ask you to take time (which may not be convenient for you) to go into a season of intercession for someone else or for some critical situation. Will you follow the King's example?

VERSE 7

You are all fair, my love,

And there is no spot in you.

The maiden is completely unveiled and totally transparent as she embraces her Beloved King, and He has found no spot in her. She is "covered in the blood" making her "white as snow." Basking in His presence has removed all the effects of sin from her life and her mind has been renewed by the Word. She is under the protection of the spiritual authority of the body of Christ as she continues to walk in servitude.

The Shulamite maiden has seen a vision of the completed work that God has purposed for her life. We all must have a vision to move toward in our spiritual walk which will motivate us to continue to run in the race. God's Word says that one will perish without a vision

Now the vision has ended and the King sees, as we will learn in the next verse, that the maiden is now ready to learn spiritual warfare.

VERSE 8

Come with me from Lebanon, my spouse,

With me from Lebanon.

Look from the top of Amana,

From the top of Senir and Hermon,

From the lions' dens,

From the mountains of the leopards.

- *Lebanon is symbolic of the Father's glory and majesty.*

- *Senir means exposure of brilliance.*

- *Amana means the secure place.*

- *Hermon means prominent precipice.*

- *Lions' dens speaks of Satan's domain.*

I Pet. 5:8 Be sober, be vigilant; because your adversary the devil walks about like a roaring lion, seeking whom he may devour. (NKJV)

- *Mountains of the leopards' dens speaks of the obstacle of spiritual forces in heavenly places.*

Before the King leaves this place of intimacy to go into a time of intercession for the maiden, He asks her to come with Him, leaving this place where they have enjoyed the Father's glory and majesty. He wants to take her with Him to a secure place on a prominent precipice; a place of brilliance, to observe and learn while He instructs her about Satan's domain and the obstacles of spiritual forces in heavenly places.

Notice that after she has seen the vision of the bridal chamber, He calls her His wife for the first time. There is still much for her to learn, however, before she is ready to take her place in the Kingdom and move into her final destiny there.

There are only subtle hints in the song alluding to Satan. Here his domain is mentioned, but Satan himself is not given much recognition in the song.

Beloved, do you place too much emphasis on the enemy of your soul? To do that gives him power to trip you in your walk! Do not make that mistake! Believe God when He says:

I John 4:4 ...He who is in you is greater than he who is in the world. (NKJV)

We should be placing our emphasis instead, beloved, on the Savior of our soul. Learn warfare as the Holy Spirit teaches you! Walk fearlessly and victoriously over the enemy's attempts to steal God's blessings from you. The enemy wants to kill the "life of God" found in your life and to destroy your effectiveness in God's Kingdom. See The Gospel of John 10:10. Satan, your enemy, will attempt to weaken your determination to lay hold of the Prize.

Let me remind you, Christian, that Jesus, your Bridegroom-King, defeated him a long time ago when he paid the bride's price of redemption on the cross. You belong to Jesus now and if you will stay focused on Him, keep your emphasis on Him, and obediently follow His instruction, neither Satan nor any of his demons will have any power over your life.

VERSE 9

You have ravished my heart,

My sister, my spouse;

You have ravished my heart

With one look of your eyes,

With one link of your necklace.

- *Ravished is to be overcome with emotions of delight because of one who is unusually beautiful, attractive, pleasing, or striking.*

Another meaning for ravish is to seize and take away by violence or to rape, plunder, or rob. The maiden has kept her eyes focused on her King in what would otherwise have been a terrifying experience for her. She followed Him, trusting in the protection of His divine authority over her as she climbed the formidable mountains of Senir, Amana, and Hermon while learning about spiritual warfare. She observed and learned from His instruction and she has now become a spiritual warrior to be reckoned with in the spiritual realm.

This maiden is now able to pursue her destiny with a violence! She has been given spiritual insight into the demonic realm that will enable her to defeat the enemy of her soul. The King brought her to this place to learn spiritual warfare because He knew that Satan and his cohorts would rob her of the Prize if she remained ignorant of their evil plans.

> Matt. 11:12 "And from the days of John the Baptist until now the kingdom of heaven suffers violence and the violent take it by force." (NKJV)

It is with this kind of tenacity that the maiden pursues her King. This action on her part has created this kind of strong emotion in her King for her. She is a little closer to grasping the Prize.

The King refers to the maiden in this verse as His wife and as His sister. She is His sister in the sense of being born again into the family of God, having the same blood flowing through her veins. A sister is born into that place in God's family, but a spouse is chosen.

In the beginning of the song, the maiden asked the King to draw her, but after failing her second test and the lessons she learned from that experience and the maturity that came into her life as a result of it, she then began to pursue the King. She embraced and held Him! It was in that embrace which she initiated where she was shown the vision of the bridal chamber – a vision of what it means to reach the Prize.

The Word says that God's people perish if they have no vision.

Prov. 29:18 Where there is no vision, the people perish... (KJ)

At this point in the song, I believe that this maiden has moved from the company of "the called" into the company of "the chosen."

Matt. 20:16 "... For many are called, but few are chosen." (NKJV)

VERSE 10

How fair is your love,

My sister, my spouse!

How much better than wine is your love

And the scent of your perfumes

Than all spices.

- *"Scent of your perfumes" are the evidences of the sanctifying (crushing) work of the Holy Spirit on one's life.*

- *Spices speaks of the various works of the Holy Spirit on our lives.*

The King now comments on the maiden's love for Him. He says her love is beautiful and transparent. She has no ulterior motives here that are hidden.

In chapter 1 verse 2, the maiden admires and desires the matchless life-transforming love of the King for His bride. The love of the King for His Bride-Queen is the Prize. Here we see that in her quest for that love, she is beginning to pour that same bridal love out on her Beloved and He admires her ability to love Him in that way. It is better than wine (which is the joy of the Holy Spirit at work in us) because that bridal love is the end result of that work.

It is interesting to note that the maturing of her bridal love begins after she sees the vision of that bridal love and is able to learn spiritual warfare in suffering love.

Perfumes of the ancient world came from plants that were crushed. Perfume is symbolic here of the Holy Spirit's sanctifying work (the crushing) which is "all spices" mentioned here. This sanctifying work in the maiden is emitting a lovely fragrance that the King is enjoying in this verse.

> **Eph. 5:2 And walk in love, as Christ also has loved us and given Himself for us, an offering and a sacrifice to God for a sweet-smelling aroma. (NKJV)**

> **II Cor. 2:14-15 Now thanks be to God who always leads us in triumph in Christ, and through us diffuses the fragrance of His knowledge in every place. For we are to God the fragrance of Christ among those who are being saved and among those who are perishing. (NKJV)**

Later in the song, we will learn more about the spices. We will learn of spices in which we are to soak; those that create the fragrance of Christ in us and which diffuses through us in every place. This perfume that our lives give off is the evidence of the Holy Spirit at work in us.

This "soaking in the spices" is a part of the preparation which transforms the maiden into that glorious Bride-Queen who will one day take her place beside the King in His Kingdom.

> **Eph. 5:26-27 that He might sanctify and cleanse her with the washing of water by the word, that He might present her to Himself a glorious church, not having spot or wrinkle or any such thing, but that she should be holy and without blemish. (NKJV)**

There is a lovely picture of this truth in the story of Esther. The maiden, Esther, soaked for one year in the fragrant oils, perfumed with spices, in her preparation before becoming the bride of the Persian King Xerxes.

VERSE 11

Your lips, O my spouse,

Drip as the honeycomb;

Honey and milk are under your tongue;

And the fragrance of your garments

Is like the fragrance of Lebanon.

- *Lips refer to receiving his intimate kisses (instruction and discipline).*

- *Drip speaks of being measures and controlled.*

- *Honeycomb is referring to the law, testimony, statutes, commandments, judgments, fear and respect of the Lord.*

In Psalms 19:7-10, we find that these are sweet as honey to the King.

**Psa. 19:10 More to be desired are they than gold,
Yea, than much fine gold;
Sweeter also than honey and the honeycomb. (NKJV)**

- *Milk is the "milk of the Word" for spiritual babes.*

- *Tongue speaks of instant or ready words.*

- *Fragrance is the "evidence of."*

- *Garments refers to "acts of service."*

- *Lebanon is symbolic of God's glory and majesty.*

The King is praising the words of the maiden. These are the words that she received from His intimate kisses which are His instructions and discipline. The Word she is speaking is the Lord's; testimonies, statutes, commandments, judgments, and the fear and respect of the Lord. Her speech is measured and controlled, not gushing, excessive, exaggerated, foolish, or unbalanced.

**Prov. 15:2 The tongue of the wise uses knowledge rightly,
But the mouth of fools pours forth foolishness. (NKJV)**

Her words feed the church in all stages of maturity and they are instant and ready.

II Tim. 4:9 Preach the word! Be ready in season and out of season. Convince, rebuke, exhort, with all longsuffering and teaching. (NKJV)

II Tim. 2:15 Be diligent to present yourself approved to God, a worker who does not need to be ashamed, rightly dividing the word of truth. (NKJV)

The Holy Spirit has now worked into her life that which the maiden had heard the King prophetically speaking over her in the vision of the bridal chamber. The King says that her acts of service are obviously born out of her time spent in God's glorious and majestic presence and he praises her!

VERSE 12

A garden enclosed

Is my sister, my spouse,

A spring shut up,

A fountain sealed.

- *Garden symbolizes one's life.*

- *Enclosed speaks of belonging to only one.*

- *Spring speaks of one's soul.*

- *Fountain speaks of one's spirit.*

A king's garden in Solomon's day provided a place of pleasure, solitude, and rest to him. It was costly and took much work and care to cultivate. The fragrances that it produced greatly pleased him and it was something he shared with his friends with great joy and delight. It was enclosed, private, and protected.

The King is saying that the maiden's life is His garden to enjoy. He admires the fact that she guards her heart's affections and her thought life, which is her soul, from the influences of the world. She keeps it just for Him. Her spirit is sealed to all others, open only to Him.

> **Is. 58:11 The Lord will guide you continually,**
> **And satisfy your soul in drought,**
> **And strengthen your bones;**
> **You shall be like a watered garden,**
> **And like a spring of water, whose waters do not fail. (NKJV)**

The maiden is learning how to hold her words until he instructs her otherwise.

> **Luke 2:19 But Mary kept all these things and pondered them in her heart. (NKJV)**

Later, in chapter 8, the maiden will express how she longs to be able to share with the church all that has been revealed to her, but she waits for His nudging.

The King is saying to her, "You are My place of refreshing, My sister, My wife. Your heart's affections and your thoughts are for Me alone and you pour out from your spirit only when I have prepared the vessel that is ready to receive it."

Her garden is another one of the secret places where intimacy with the King is shared.

VERSE 13

Your plants are an orchard of pomegranates

With pleasant fruits,

Fragrant henna with spikenard,

- *Plants speaks of spiritual growth.*

- *Orchard speaks of a multitude.*
- *Fruits are love, joy, peace, kindness, goodness, longsuffering, faithfulness, gentleness, and self-control as found in Galatians 5:22-23.*

- *Fragrant is the "evidence of."*

- *Henna speaks of being transformed into His image.*

- *Spikenard is symbolic of true praise and worship.*

The King sees much spiritual growth in the priestly character of the maiden. He also sees the fruit of the spirit in her life and He sees evidence that she is being transformed into His image through her praise and worship. True worship is a work of the Holy Spirit.

Spikenard is a rare, costly spice. It is one of the spices which are considered to be the various works of the Holy Spirit in one's life.

VERSE 14

Spikenard and saffron,

Calamus and cinnamon,

With all trees of frankincense,

Myrrh and aloes,

With all the chief spices—

- *Spikenard is true praise and worship.*

- *Saffron is faith.*

- *Calamus is doing what is right in God's sight.*

- *Cinnamon is holiness of heart.*

- *Frankincense is intercession.*

- *Myrrh is suffering love or sacrificial love.*

- *Aloes speaks of the intimate closeness between the King and His Father to her.*

John 14:20 "At that day you will know that I am in My Father, and you are in Me, and I in you." (NKJV)

- *Chief spices are all the various works of the Holy Spirit in one's life.*

These are some of the things that the King sees here – that the Holy Spirit is working in the maiden's life.

VERSE 15

A fountain of gardens,

A well of living waters,

And streams from Lebanon.

The King is speaking prophetically here as He proclaims the finished work that He sees in this Shulamite maiden. The finished work that He sees is a continuous flow of the Holy Spirit pouring into her life – that which comes from the very glory and majesty of God. This flow of the Holy Spirit is producing a depth of maturity in the maiden that is springing up and pouring out into the lives of all those around her.

Compare this verse with verse 12 of this chapter. In verse 12, the King saw the maiden as a garden enclosed and His alone to enjoy. Now we see a progression from a garden enclosed to a fountain of gardens where the maiden is reproducing the good things that are in her garden (or her life) in the lives of others. This is evangelism and discipleship.

Whereas the King proclaimed her a fountain sealed, He now sees a well of living water. She will become a refreshing, life-giving source from which all can drink.

While she was a spring shut up (closed), He now sees streams from Lebanon where a flow of the Holy Spirit is coming into her life from the glory and majesty of God. That stream flows out of her life to bless others.

VERSE 16

THE SHULAMITE

Awake, O north wind,

And come, O south!

Blow upon my garden,

That its spices may flow out.

Let my beloved come to his garden

And eat its pleasant fruits.

- *North wind is the cold wind of trials.*

- *South wind is the warm wind of blessings.*

The maiden now calls on the cold north wind of trials and the warm south wind of blessings to blow over her life because she knows that both are needed in order for her to produce fruit... She knows that the work of the Holy Spirit in her life must be tested so that her faith will be strong and fruitful.

She invites her Beloved to come into her garden (her life), which she now proclaims is His garden, and be refreshed by the good things that He might find there. She is His to take pleasure in. Hers is a life that gives off the fragrance of Christ, no matter what the circumstances are of her life – trials or blessings. We see her emphasis being placed less and less on herself and her needs as she begins to express a desire to minister to the needs of her Beloved.

In this chapter from beginning to end, the King has lavished affirming words of admiration upon the maiden. Our Beloved Bridegroom, King Jesus, feels the same way about you and me and we need to know it. Why? Because when we begin to understand and accept how He sees us, we begin to lose our insecurities. We begin to focus less on ourselves and our selfish desires. Instead we focus more on Jesus and His interests.

John 3:30 He must increase, but I must decrease. (NKJV)

CHAPTER FOUR REVIEW

1. Those for whom the maiden is responsible to God are represented by _____

_____

2. Those in Jesus' flock who serve and give of themselves are represented by _____

_____

3. Pomegranates are symbolic of _____

_____

4. When the King sees that the maiden is prepared to do His will, He compares her to __

_____

5. The gazelle represents what? _____

_____

6. Myrrh and frankincense represent what? _____

_____

7. The evidence of the work of the Holy Spirit is represented by _____

_____

8. Fragrance refers to what? _____

_____

9. Spikenard is a costly perfume that represents what? _____

_____

10. The south wind represents what? _____

_____

CHAPTER FIVE

CHASTISEMENT

VERSE 1

THE BELOVED

I have come to my garden, my sister my, spouse;

I have gathered my myrrh with my spice;

I have eaten my honeycomb with my honey;

I have drunk my wine with my milk.

(To his friends):

Eat, O friends!

Drink, yes, drink deeply,

O beloved ones!

- *Garden represents one's life.*

- *Myrrh speaks of suffering love or sacrificial love.*

- *Spice is the various administrations of the Holy Spirit in one's life.*

- *Honeycomb with honey speaks of the substance of the sweet fruit produced in one's life as a result of acting on the Word of God.*

- *Wine is the joy of the Holy Spirit at work in one's life.*

- *Milk is the elementary principles of God's Word.*

Notice that the Beloved refers to the maiden now as His sister. She gave Him total and complete Lordship of her life in the last verse of the previous chapter. He refers to her as His sister because she has been born again into His family and as His spouse because He has chosen her to be His Bride-Queen.

The self-sacrificial love that she demonstrates to Him and to others in her life ministers to Him. (Myrrh)

The joy of the various administrations of the Holy Spirit working in her life ministers to Him. (Spice) (Wine)

The substance of the sweet fruit from acting on the Word being produced in her life ministers to Him. (Honeycomb/honey)

Her willingness to teach and disciple spiritual babes in the elementary principles of the Word also ministers to Him. (Milk)

All of these things nurture and refresh the Bridegroom King. He demonstrates His full ownership of her by allowing others to be nurtured and refreshed as well in His garden by her life.

Christian, do you realize that you are a garden for your Bridegroom, Jesus, to enjoy? Do you realize that all of the things mentioned above, if they are operable in your life, minister to Him?

This relationship that we enjoy with our Lord works both ways. We can nurture and refresh Jesus as well as be nurtured and refreshed by Him.

VERSE 2

THE SHULAMITE

I sleep, but my heart is awake;

It is the voice of my beloved!

He knocks, saying,

"Open for me, my sister, my love,

My dove, my perfect one;

For my head is covered with dew,

My locks with drops of the night.

The scene changes once again. Evidently some time has passed since the garden experience and the maiden is back in her bedroom. It seems that she has become comfortable and complacent once again.

There is a battle taking place in her soul between her mind and her heart. Her mind has been lulled into a lethargic state. Evidently she has been listening again to her brothers. Her heart's affections are still on her Beloved but it has been too long since she has spent intimate time with Him. Now she has become closed and unavailable to Him. We will see that she has reverted to her old legalistic thought patterns in the next verse. This deadly mind set will hinder the work of the Holy Spirit in one's life; however, she is still able to hear and discern His voice.

- *His head speaks of leadership.*

- *His locks speak of dedication.*

- *"Drops of the night" speaks of a long struggle through a dark, hard time of suffering.*

Her Beloved has just returned from a Gethsemane experience and He is knocking at the closed door of her heart, seeking entrance into His garden to be nurtured and refreshed. He expresses His love for her and encourages her with words of affirmation (referring to her as His love, His perfect one).

In all of the other verses of the song, when the Beloved is speaking to the Shulamite, He refers to her as being fair (unveiled and available to Him). However, in this verse, the maiden is evidently veiled to Him, her Husband. She is treating Him like a stranger. This maiden who had asked to run with Him and had asked Him to draw her unto Himself in intimacy in the first chapter of this song is now unavailable to Him. Remember that she had given the King full ownership of her life in chapter 4.

II Cor. 3:18 But we all with <u>unveiled</u> face, beholding as in a mirror the glory of the Lord, are being transformed into the same image... (NKJV)
(underscore added for emphasis)

I believe that at this point in the maiden's journey, she is facing her third test. It is what the King referred to in verse 6 of chapter 4 when he spoke of another dark time to come. You will remember that He left their place of intimacy to go to meet the challenge of suffering love and intercession on her behalf, demonstrating the traits of a dedicated leader. He has returned now from this "Gethsemane" experience to visit the maiden to strengthen and encourage her and to be refreshed by her, only to find His garden closed and locked to Him.

VERSE 3

I have taken off my robe;

How can I put it on again?

I have washed my feet;

How can I defile them?

- *Robe represents her strength and honor.*

Prov. 31:25 Strength and honor are her clothing; (NKJV)

The maiden's strength comes from drawing apart and spending time in intimate fellowship with the King. Her honor comes from running with Him in ministry. The maiden says that she has laid this aside and she doesn't know how to put them on again.

The last portion of this verse lets us know that she has become more concerned with the letter of the law than with her Beloved's needs, and this has caused her to become indifferent to the needs of others as well. I would say that she is in danger of becoming "lukewarm," a dangerous condition to be in for the bride of a King.

> **Rom. 7:4 Therefore, my brethren, you also have become dead to the law through the body of Christ, that you may be married to another – to Him who was raised from the dead, that we should bear fruit for God. (NKJV)**

Christian, let us take a lesson here from the maiden. We must never allow anyone to mislead us into thinking that we can:

1. Ignore the importance of drawing apart in intimacy with our Beloved.

2. Neglect our commitment to answer His call to servitude in the body of Christ when He summons us.

VERSE 4

My beloved put his hand

By the latch of the door,

And my heart yearned for him.

- *His hand is His will in action.*

- *The door represents the entrance to one's heart. The heart is the seat of one's emotions and intimacy.*

- *The latch represents one's freedom of choice. Only the maiden can choose to open the door to her heart.*

Complacency and indifference toward the King, due to a legalistic approach to the Word, had locked the door of the maiden's heart that gave the King access to intimacy with her. The King owns this garden but He will not force His way into it. His will, active at this point in the song, is that the maiden spend intimate time alone with Him. He longs to enter her garden and to be refreshed. The maiden's heart is in tune with the King's will, but her mind is polluted with "stinkin' thinkin'!" There is a battle raging on the battlefield of her soul between her heart and her mind.

Jesus went to Gethsemane and endured the cross with love for His Bride ever before Him and foremost in His mind.

> **Heb. 12:2b ...who for the joy that was set before Him endured the cross, despising the shame, and has sat down at the right hand of the throne of God. (NKJV)**

I believe that the joy which was set before Jesus, in this verse of the scripture, was a vision of the glorious, spotless bride of Christ.

Christian, right now our beloved Bridegroom King is at the right hand of the throne of God where He awaits His bride, His glorious bride, who has prepared herself to take her place beside Him in God's Kingdom.

Is it any wonder that myrrh (suffering, sacrificial love) dripped from the latch of the maiden's door, upon which her Beloved's hand had rested while He stood waiting. He was waiting at the door that separated them. Only she could open the door. I cannot imagine the pain and suffering that He must have felt at her resistance; a pain even greater than that of Gethsemane. Knowing that His glorious bride awaited Him was what helped Him to endure that Gethsemane experience and how it must have broken His heart that she would not avail herself now to a time of intimate fellowship with Him.

Saints of God, how many times have we made excuses and resisted the wooing of the Bridegroom when He was calling us to rise up and come away – to draw apart from our busy lifestyle and spend intimate time alone with Him?

VERSE 5

I arose to open for my beloved,

And my hands dripped with myrrh,

My fingers with liquid myrrh,

On the handles of the lock.

- *My hands symbolizes her will in action.*

- *Myrrh symbolizes suffering, sacrificial love.*

The maiden's heart won out over her mind and she sets her will in action to open for her Beloved. She takes her legalistic thoughts captive to the obedience of Christ and overcomes her lukewarm state. She rises up to open the door of her heart to a time of intimacy with the King. Her Beloved's demonstration of suffering in sacrificial love has helped her to get her thinking back on track.

VERSE 6

I opened for my beloved,

But my beloved had turned away and was gone.

My heart leaped up when he spoke.

I sought him, but I could not find him,

I called him, but he gave me no answer.

The maiden waited too long and once again the King has removed His manifested presence. Her heart of love for Him responded to His voice, but her mind held her back and she missed the moment.

Will she give in now, give up and go back to her complacency and indifference? Will she return to her lukewarm state?

> **Rev. 3:16-22 "So then, because you are lukewarm, and neither cold nor hot, I will vomit you out of my mouth.**
> **17 "Because you say, "I am rich, have become wealthy, and have need of nothing" – and do not know that you are wretched, miserable, poor, blind, and naked—**
> **18 "I counsel you to buy from Me gold refined in the fire, that you may be rich, and white garments, that you may be clothed, that the shame of**

your nakedness may not be revealed; and anoint your eyes with eye
salve, that you may see.
19 "As many as I love, I rebuke and chasten. Therefore be zealous and
repent.
20 "Behold, I stand at the door and knock, if anyone hears My voice and
opens the door, I will come in to him and dine with him, and he with Me.
21 "To him who overcomes, I will grant to sit with Me on My throne, as I
also overcame and sat down with My Father on His throne.
22 "He who has an ear, let him hear what the Spirit says to the
churches." "" (NKJV)

The King loves the maiden too much to let her remain in this dangerous state, so He draws her out of this place once again by removing His manifested presence. He knows that her heart of love for Him will cause her to seek after Him, and the discipline and chastisement can begin!

Christian, we must take a lesson from the maiden's experience here. We must beware of the leaven of the Pharasees. Jesus warned us in Matthew 16:6 and 12 to beware of man's legalistic interpretation of the Word with out the divine interpretation of the Holy Spirit.

> **Matt. 16:6 Then Jesus said to them, "Take heed and beware of the leaven
> of the Pharasees and the Sadduccees."**
> **12 Then they understood that He did not tell them to beware of the
> leaven of bread, but of the doctrine of the Pharasees and the Sadduccees.**
> **(NKJV)**

Please understand that leaven, or a legalistic approach to the Word, may affect your walk with the Lord. Let me ask you, "Would you rather have a religious man's interpretation of the scripture, or the Holy Spirit's enlightenment of God's Word?"

We are fighting an all out war with the enemy. Jesus has provided all we need in order to be victorious. We must seek Him and His counsel provided by the Holy Spirit's enlightenment of God's Word if we are to win over the enemy. Simply put, our Christian walk is not a religion, but it is a relationship with Jesus.

I believe it is absolutely essential that we keep our focus continuously on Jesus and on Him alone as we walk through our life's song. He is our way through the perils of this life to our salvation and to the Prize, the goal of the upward call of God in Christ Jesus.

> **Gal. 5:1, 4, 7-9 Stand fast therefore in the liberty by which Christ has
> made free, and do not be entangled again with a yoke of bondage.**
> **4 You have become estranged from Christ, you who attempt to be
> justified by law; you have fallen from grace.**
> **7 You ran well. Who hindered you from obeying the truth?**
> **8 This persuasion does not come from Him who calls you.**
> **9 A little leaven leavens the whole lump.**

VERSE 7

The watchmen who went about the city found me.

They struck me, they wounded me;

The keepers of the walls

Took my veil away from me.

- *Watchmen represent the God appointed leaders who guard and watch over the church in the world and point all to Jesus.* (I Timothy 5:17 and I Peter 5:1-5)

- *City is symbolic of worldliness.*

- *"Keepers of the walls" represent those of the watchmen to whom one is to be personally accountable.*

- *Walls are symbolic of one's determination.*

- *Veil is symbolic of servitude in and through the body of Christ and it says to the world that one belongs to Jesus.*

The watchmen of chapter three, who found the maiden during her struggle to find her Beloved, find her again in the same condition. This time she is severely chastised by the God appointed leaders who watch over the affairs of the church out in the world.

Worldliness has no place in a Christian's life!

> **Prov. 27:5-6 Open rebuke is better than love carefully concealed. Faithful are the wounds of a friend, but the kisses of an enemy are deceitful. (NKJV)**

> **Heb. 12:5-6 ..."My son, do not despise the chastening of the Lord, nor be discouraged when you are rebuked by Him. For whom the Lord loves He chastens, and scourges every son whom He receives." (NKJV)**

The maiden had determined early in chapter one to run with her King in ministry and she had asked Him to draw her in intimacy to receive His kisses. Now the keepers of the walls are holding her accountable and they have confronted her behavior.

This is the maiden who, in chapter three, had carried her Beloved into the church, testifying and encouraging those in the church to draw closer to the King in intimacy and to run with Him in ministry – the very thing she had failed to do. Instead, she had demonstrated a selfish, self-serving attitude and a lifestyle of indifference to the King's interests and needs. This is a common malady in one who allows a legalistic approach to the scriptures to influence them as the maiden has done at this point in the song.

In confronting her behavior, the keepers of the walls removed her veil. This caused her to realize that she had damaged her witness to both others in the church and to those in the world. It damaged the effectiveness of her servitude within the body of Christ. The keepers of the walls have brought to her attention that she was bought with a price and that she belongs to her King. She gave her life to Him and she is His garden now and not her own.

I Cor. 6:20 For you were bought at a price; therefore glorify God in your body and in your spirit, which are God's. (NKJV)

VERSE 8

I charge you, O daughters of Jerusalem,

If you find my beloved,

That you tell him I am lovesick.

The Shulamite does not become bitter, discouraged, or defeated; neither does she isolate herself from the church. She humbly goes to her support group in the body of Christ and she asks them to help her to find her way back into the King's manifested presence. She asks them to intercede for her because she finds that she loves Him now more than ever.

...and the lovely wounded maiden begins to.. worship...

VERSE 9

THE DAUGHTERS OF JERUSALEM

What is your beloved

More than another beloved,

O fairest among women?

What is your beloved

More than another beloved,

That you so charge us?

In this verse we see some insight into the bride company. The discipline of the watchmen does not cause the daughters to reject the bride's efforts to restore her place in His presence. The maiden has sought them out and now she receives their administrations. They provoke her to love by asking her questions that cause her to examine her heart and that help to get her refocused.

Heb. 10:24 And let us consider one another in order to stir up (provoke) love and good works. (NKJV)

The bride company, like the Beloved, encourages her with affirming words of faith by referring to her as "fairest among women." Whereas the maiden was veiled and unavailable in verse two, now she is once again unveiled, vulnerable, and transparent not just to the King, but to them as well. In her dark hour of the humiliation of failure, their question forces her to focus once again on her Beloved rather than on herself and her circumstances...

...And the lovely, wounded maiden begins to worship!

VERSE 10

THE SHULAMITE

My beloved is white and ruddy.

Chief among ten thousand.

- *White speaks of purity and the radiance of God's glory.*

- *Ruddy is earthy, approachable, easy to be with, robust, and healthy.*
- *Chief is superior to all others.*

- *Ten thousand is representative of a seed in the image of God through the fullness of testing.[5]*

The Shulamite, in her dark hour, begins to pour out her heart for the King as she refocuses on him and begins to express His attributes in worship.

As she begins to worship in response to the severe chastisement she has received from the watchmen, by studying her behavior, we will each be empowered to be an extravagant worshiper. It will help to make us into one who will worship in spirit and in truth in the midst of the bad circumstances as well as the good circumstances. That is what a true worshiper does!

> **John 4:23 "But the hour is coming, and now is, when the true worshipers will worship the Father in spirit and truth, for the Father is seeking such to worship Him." (NKJV)**

In this and the next five verses, we are given a glorious description of our Bridegroom King as He was in the Kingdom before he left it to come and rescue His bride. It also describes how He must appear now as He awaits the day when His bride queen will be revealed.

Here we see another paradox when the maiden says that her Beloved is white and ruddy. The maiden is declaring, in her worship, that her Beloved is pure and radiant with God's glory and at the same time he is robustly healthy, earthy, approachable, and easy to be with. Her Beloved is fully God and fully man! She declares that He is incomparably superior to all other men. He is the first fruit of many men and women who will become like God through the fullness of testing.

VERSE 11

His head is like the finest gold;

His locks are wavy,

And black as a raven.

- *Head is symbolic of sovereign leadership*

- *Gold is symbolic of God's divine nature.*

- *Locks speak of dedication to God.*

    - *Wavy and black speak of the strength and vitality of youth.*

---

[5] "Numbers in Scripture" by E. W. Bullinger.

- *Raven is symbolic of God's provision.*

Luke 12:24 "Consider the ravens, for they neither sow nor reap, which have neither storehouse nor barn; and God feeds them. Of how much more value are you than the birds?" (NKJV)

The King's sovereign leadership over all of creation is divinely superb – it is like God's leadership. Jesus said in His word that He only did what He saw His Father do. His dedication to God and to His church is with the strength and vitality of youth as He looks to God to supply it.

VERSE 12

His eyes are like doves

By the rivers of waters,

Washed with milk

And fitly set.

- *Doves eyes speaks of singleness of vision.*

- *Rivers of waters speaks of overwhelming purity, transparency; clear and clean.*

- *Milk speaks of the elementary principles of the Word, the simple spiritual food for new Christians.*

- *Fitly set speaks of order, integrity, truth, and clarity.*

The King's eyes, like doves' eyes, have singleness of vision. They are focused on His Father and His Father's interests.

John 5:19 Then Jesus answered and said to them, "Most assuredly, I say to you, the Son can do nothing of Himself, but what He sees the Father do: for whatever He does, the Son also does in like manner." (NKJV)

His eyes see with pure transparency. He views us through the simple principles of the Word with insight into every dark secret, yet with integrity, truth, and clarity, as God sees. Nothing is hidden in us from the scrutiny of His gaze and yet He remains pure, innocent, and holy.

Rev. 2:18, 23 ...the Son of God, who has eyes like a flame of fire ... all the churches shall know that I am He who searches the minds and hearts. (NKJV)

John 2:24-25 But Jesus did not commit himself to them, because He knew all men, and had no need that anyone should testify of man, for He knew what was in man. (NKJV)

Child of God, when we position ourselves in a place of intimate fellowship with our Beloved, we know that we will be transparent and vulnerable to the scrutiny of His gaze. This is why, much like the maiden, we sometimes hesitate or avoid the call of our Beloved to draw apart in intimacy with Him.

VERSE 13

His cheeks are like a bed of spices,

Banks of scented herbs.

His lips are lilies,

Dripping liquid myrrh.

- *Cheeks are symbolic of one's emotions.*

- *Bed of spices is symbolic of the various works of the Holy Spirit in the corporate bride.*

- *Scented herbs symbolize the evidence of healing and health; obvious divine health.*

- *Banks speaks of abundance.*

- *Lips speaks of intimacy.*

- *Lilies refers to the bride-queen of Christ.*

- *Dripping speaks of consistency, measured and controlled.*

- *Liquid speaks of a flowing.*

- *Myrrh is symbolic of suffering or sacrificial love.*

The King's heart, the seat of His emotions, toward the corporate bride-queen is to see the various administrations of the Holy Spirit at work in her, which brings the pleasant evidence of abundant healing and health flowing consistently in her life. He passionately desires this for His bride-queen. He consistently demonstrates sacrificial love toward those who are moving nearer to their destiny as His bride-queen, He is eager to share His intimate kisses with them.

His intimate kisses (the discipline and instruction) produce the mature bride who consistently dies to her flesh. This demonstrates suffering or self-sacrificial love. This demonstration of sacrificial love flows out of His life and into the life of the bride company. From them it flows into the lives of others.

VERSE 14

His hands are rods of gold

Set with beryl.

His body is carved ivory

Inlaid with sapphires.

- *Hands are symbolic of one's will in action.*

- *Rod is symbolic of authority.*

- *Gold is symbolic of God's divine nature.*

- *Beryl speaks of fullness of testing, through which the new creation will be completed.*

- *His body speaks of the body of Christ.*

- *Carved speaks of transformation.*

- *Ivory symbolizes a pure throne and royalty.*

- *Inlaid speaks of being placed or set in a place; to rest.*

- *Sapphire is symbolic of God's manifested presence.*

This verse says to me that the King's will in action is carried out with divine authority. His will is that the new creation will be completed through the fullness of testing. That new creation makes up his body, the body of Christ, and it will be transformed into a pure royal throne that God's manifested presence will rest in and on.

Saints of God, if you have embraced servitude under the authority of His body, the body of Christ, then you carry God's manifested presence in your life as you serve. You actually are His hands and His feet in the world we live in today.

VERSE 15

His legs are pillars of marble

Set on bases of fine gold.

His countenance is like Lebanon,

Excellent as the cedars.

- *Legs symbolize one's walk; the administration of one's purposes.*

- *Pillars speak of the overcomer.*

- *Marble speaks of strength; it is durable and permanent.*

- *Bases speak of foundations.*

- *Gold symbolizes God's divine nature.*

- *Countenance speaks of impartation and favor.*

- *Lebanon is symbolic of God's majesty and glory.*

- *Cedars speaks of righteousness; right standing with God.*

The King's purposes are strongly established on the foundation of God's divine nature. His purposes or plans overcome all others and are durable and permanent. They will prevail
His impartation to her is God's majesty and glory resting upon her life and right standing with God.

VERSE 16

His mouth is most sweet,

Yes, he is altogether lovely.

This is my beloved,

And this is my friend,

O daughters of Jerusalem!

- *Mouth is symbolic of speech; speaking the word.*

The King's speech (His words) is sweet to her. Yes, the Shulamite maiden loves everything she understands, at this point, about her Beloved and His Word.

She proclaims to the bride company, "My Beloved is the lover of my soul and my friend." She not only loves everything about Him but she even likes Him. She is safe, fulfilled, and comfortable in their relationship, even though she is challenged to leave her comfort zone in order to follow after Him.

The King has been silent during this time of darkest night in her soul. He continues to remain quiet ... and the church watches.

The maiden is wounded and exposed to all in her humiliation. She is transparent and vulnerable. She could have stubbornly remained in her complacent, indifferent, and legalistic state of mind; safe in her room behind locked doors and away from anything or anyone that threatened her secure position.

But she did not have the Prize! In order to have the Prize, she had to leave that nice, comfortable place and seek after her Beloved. So the maiden suffered the wounds of the watchmen and the confrontation of the keepers of the wall in order to find her way back into her Beloved's manifested presence.

Now the maiden worships in the midst of these adverse circumstances as the whole world watches!

This kind of holy abandonment in worship, as one focuses on Jesus during the darkest night of one's soul, is one of the things that God will use to awaken the church in the earth before His return!

CHAPTER FIVE REVIEW

1. How can the Shulamite maiden be both "sister" and "spouse?" _____

_____

2. When the maiden says she has taken off her robe, what is she saying? _____

_____

3. What action locked the maiden's heart? _____

_____

4. The leaven of the Pharasees and Sadduccees represents _____

_____

5. Who are the "Keepers of the walls?" _____

_____

6. How do the daughters of Jerusalem help the maiden to regain her place in her Beloved's

manifested presence? _____

_____

7. The purity and radiance of God's glory are represented by _____

_____

8. The spiritual food for new Christians is represented by _____

_____

9. The word, carved, refers to a _____

_____

10. Durable and permanent strength is represented by _____

_____

CHAPTER SIX

RESTORED

VERSE 1

THE DAUGHTERS OF JERUSALEM

Where has your beloved gone,

O fairest among women?

Where has your beloved turned aside,

That we may seek him with you?

The daughters of Jerusalem speak again and they ask another question to help the maiden get back on track. They help her to remember the garden experience of chapter five, verse one. They are committed to helping her find her way back into the Beloved's manifested presence. They see her as the Beloved sees her – as most beautiful. They see that she is now unveiled and available to Him. It is not the maiden's circumstances upon which the bride company is looking; rather, it is her heart for the Beloved that they see.

Saints of God, are we as willing to look past the circumstances of one who may be struggling in their life's song, to lift them up to Jesus for restoration and healing?

Notice in the second question of this verse that the bride company speaks of seeking the Beloved Bridegroom King with the maiden.

Christian, we will never get to a place in our walk where we do not seek after our lovely Lord. He is constantly moving and in order for us to stay focused on Him, we must move with Him. We continually seek after Him – **seeking Him first.** We seek him first about all the things that concern our lives, our marriages, our homes, our churches, our jobs, our communities, and situations in our world.

> **Matt. 6:33 "But seek first the kingdom of God and His righteousness,
> and all these things shall be added to you." (NKJV)**

> **Isa. 55:6 "Seek the Lord while he may be found,
> Call upon him while He is near." (NKJV)**

Yes, the bride company continually pursues the King with a passion and a fervor that will not be daunted.

VERSE 2

THE SHULAMITE

My beloved has gone to his garden,

To the beds of spices,

To feed his flock in the garden,

And to gather lilies.

- *"Bed of spices" refers to those in the corporate worldwide body of Christ who are allowing the Holy Spirit's various administrations to transform them.*

- *Lilies are symbolic of the bride-queen.*

As the maiden considers the bride company's question, she remembers the King's pleasure. His pleasure is to dwell much in the lives of those in the corporate body who are allowing the Holy Spirit's various administrations to transform them. They minister to and refresh the shepherd King and His flock from their garden (their lives) and the King gathers His bride-queen from those gardens.

As she remembers, her passion for the King is stirred and she is encouraged to return and restore her place of servanthood within the body of Christ.

VERSE 3

I am my beloved's

And my beloved is mine.

He feeds his flock among the lilies.

The Shulamite is back on track! She is after the Prize and refocused on her Beloved and their relationship.

Nothing has changed, however, from the instruction that she was given in the first chapter of the song. She wants the King to feed and satisfy her so that she can mature into a bride who is able to take her place at His side in the Kingdom. For this to happen, she must find Him from within the body of Christ and follow in the footsteps of the flock. In doing this, she is learning servitude to Him and to others along with the rest of the bride company.

In verse sixteen of chapter two, the maiden says, "My Beloved is mine, and I am His." She is placing the emphasis in this relationship on herself first. In this verse, we see the maiden's emphasis shifting. Now it is placed on the King first and we are given some insight into the heart of the maiden.

Matt. 12:34b-35a "...out of the abundance of the heart the mouth speaks. A good man out of the good treasure of his heart brings forth good things..." (NKJV)

The maiden is remembering the prophetic words that her Beloved spoke over her at the beginning of chapter two:

"Like a lily among thorns, so is my love..."

She remembers that the King's habit is to spend much time gathering lilies from His garden – for Jesus has come, beloved, to rescue His bride-queen out of this cursed world. She remembers that her Beloved feeds His flock there among the lilies and her passion is stirred.

VERSE 4

THE BELOVED

O my love, you are as beautiful as Tirzah,

Lovely as Jerusalem,

Awesome as an army with banners!

- *Tirzah means "delightfully beautiful" and "she is friendly."*

It was a very sinful Canaanite city in the northern kingdom before it was captured by Israel and it was so named because of its remarkable natural beauty.

- *Jerusalem means peace.*

Jerusalem was the capitol of Israel and the place of Solomon's temple where God's manifested glory was. It was a city known for its spiritual beauty. It is referred to as the "bride of Christ" in Rev. 21:2, 9-10.

To see the beautiful city of Jerusalem in a setting of harsh rocky terrain causes me to think of the King's statement in verse two of chapter two once again, when he refers to the maiden as a "lily among thorns." This is to say that she is a **pure** bride in the **cursed** earth.

The King finally reveals Himself and He speaks, after a long silence, in response to her extravagant worship of Him. He begins to reaffirm her by expressing to her His admiration of her inward and outward beauty and He lets her know that their friendship is intact.

Child of God, Jesus' love for us is stronger than our weaknesses. He believes in you and in me and He calls us friend.

> **John 15:15 "... but I have called you friends, for all things that I heard from My Father I have made known to you." (NKJV)**

Healthy, strong marriages, in my opinion, are those where the couples are not only lovers but best friends.

The King's stubborn love has drawn the maiden to Himself through this time of testing and He proclaims that she is a victorious warrior. She had struggled, but has now overcome, resulting in the defeat of the enemy of her soul – the enemy that would prevent her from laying hold of the Prize!

VERSE 5

Turn your eyes away from me,

For they have overcome me.

Your hair is like a flock of goats

Going down from Gilead.

- *Hair is symbolic of our separation unto God.*

- *Gilead means perpetual testimony.*

The maiden had become sidetracked; her focus had not been on the King but on her brothers. As a result, she found herself going through another dark, hard time because she had miserably failed her third test.

The King is not rebuking her in this verse. He is overcome with her faithful, loving pursuit of Him as she walks through the humiliation of this hard time in her life. Her determination to remain separated unto God is a perpetual testimony to all.

Jesus is totally overcome by weak, broken people who love Him in the midst of trials and failures. It has been said that our worship is His greatest weakness!

I believe that the intensity of the King's love for the maiden so overwhelms Him, seeing her in this state, that He is tempted to sweep her away from her circumstances rather than to allow her to face this hard time. In the later part of this verse, He sees that, as a result of facing this hard time, she is once again strong in her commitment to God; and she is strong in her determination to run in ministry with Him. She is determined to shepherd and care for the flock for which she is responsible. The very virtues which He saw and spoke prophetically over the maiden in chapter four have matured in her life through the fullness of testing and are seen in the testimony of her actions.

VERSE 6

Your teeth are like a flock of sheep

Which have come up from the washing;

Every one bears twins,

And none is barren among them.

- *Teeth symbolizes the ability to digest the meat of the word.*

- *Come up speaks of promotion.*

- *Twins speaks of balance.*
- *Not barren speaks of fruitfulness.*

The King sees that the maiden is now able to digest and rightly handle the Word of truth as she serves while following Him. "Coming up from the washing" is saying that she is being promoted by the washing of the water of the Word in her life. She has a healthy balance of the Word and that balance is producing good fruit in her.

> **Eph. 5:25-26 "Husbands, love your wives, just as Christ also loved the church and gave Himself for her, that He might sanctify and cleanse her with the washing of water by the word." (NKJV)**

> **II Tim. 2:15 Be diligent (study) to present yourself approved to God, a worker who does not need to be ashamed, rightly dividing the word of truth. (NKJV)**

VERSE 7

Like a piece of pomegranate

Are your temples behind your veil.

- *Pomegranate is symbolic of the priesthood.*

- *Temples refers to one's thought life.*

The King sees that the maiden's mind is being renewed, and her thought life has become pure and Godly as she digests to meat of the Word. The prophetic Words He spoke over her in verse three of chapter four have come to fruition. She is of the royal priesthood and her thought life is indicative of that fact. She does not let her mind dwell on ungodly thoughts – instead those thoughts are taken captive to the obedience of Christ.

> **II Cor. 10:5 ... and we take captive every thought to make it obedient to Christ. (NIV)**

The veil, which the keepers of the walls took from her in chapter five, has now been returned to her and she has been reinstated into her place of servitude in the body of Christ. This place of servitude within the life of the church becomes a testimony of the overcoming power of God in her life to all who observe her journey.

VERSES 8-9

There are sixty queens

And eighty concubines,

And virgins without number.

My dove, my perfect one,

Is the only one,

The only one of her mother,

The favorite of the one who bore her,

The daughters saw her

And called her blessed,

The queens and the concubines,

And they praised her.

The people mentioned here in these two verses are all Kingdom citizens within the life of the church that are in various relationships to the King.

- *Queens are those who have had the fullness of testing. They have run the race and they have reached the prize.*

This is a Kingdom term:

6 = the number of man
10 = fullness of testing.

- *Concubines refer to those who have begun to be tested, and because of it, they have quit running the race.*

They are no longer pursuing the Prize because it's "just too hard." They tend to be content to just settle for a self pleasing church/palace lifestyle.

8 = new beginnings
10 = fullness of testing (#7)

- *Virgins speaks of those who have not accepted other suitors.*

They have not yet entered into a covenant of marriage with the King either – a covenant that keeps them for Him alone. They love the mention of His name but they are not born again.

- ***The one who bore her speaks of her mother, the church.***

- ***The daughters are all others in the world.***

The King is saying that these, who are mentioned in their various relationships to him, all favor, bless, and praise the maiden because she is still in the race. She is actively pursuing an intimate, life transforming relationship with the King – her eyes are on Him and she is still after the Prize and will not stop short of it!

VERSE 10

Who is she who looks forth as the morning,

Fair as the moon,

Clear as the sun,

Awesome as an army with banners.

This verse, in my opinion, is one of the most incredible verses in the song. The King is speaking now, not just to the characters in this scene of the song, but to the church down through the ages of time. He is speaking to you and me!

- *Moon is symbolic of the pure church that reflects the sun.*

- *Sun is symbolic of Jesus, the Word.*

He is asking, "Who is the one who will meet bravely the challenges of the dark night of testing with hope and trust? Who will be veiled to the world but always unveiled and beautifully transparent before Me? Who will be a light that shines in the dark night of others, to encourage them while pointing all to Me? Who will be a victorious warrior who is awesome in her overcoming power against the enemy of her soul"?

Will it be you --- will it be me?

This is a mystery hidden in the pages of the song and it is like a treasure map for us to follow.

The Shulamite maiden is showing you and me in this, the Song of all Songs, the proper path for out life's journey. We must take this path in order to become that **"perfect and only one"** who will lay hold of the Prize – **the matchless, life changing love of the King for His bride!** She is showing us how to reach our destiny. It is what we must do if we are to take our place as Jesus' glorious bride-queen in God's kingdom!

VERSE 11

THE SHULAMITE

I went down to the garden of nuts

To see the verdure of the valley,

To see whether the vine had budded

And the pomegranates had bloomed

- *The "garden of nuts" speaks of the lives of those souls who have a dark, hard shell around them, yet with delicious fruit on the inside when the shell is crushed.*

- *The vine is in reference to the church.*

- *The valley speaks of that place of complacency or indifference.*

- *Budding speaks of potential fruit.*

- *Pomegranates speak of the priesthood.*

- *Verdure is the greenness of growing vegetation, a condition of health and vigor.[6]*

The maiden has rolled her sleeves up to go to work! She has gone down to the souls of those in the church who are in the valley of complacency and indifference in their walk but have the potential to produce much fruit in their lives. These people are at the same places where she had been on several occasions in her life's song, when her Beloved came and brought her out. Now she is doing for others what the King did for her. She is watching over the interests (the church) of her Beloved to encourage the priesthood to keep their minds renewed in the Word and to keep their thought-life pure.

Notice that the maiden has left the comforts of her safe place. She is no longer resting evasively in her complacency which was undermining her determination to run with her Beloved. She has grown past her failures. She has come to know and believe what the King has been seeing and speaking over her all along. She is no longer preoccupied with the "letter of the law" that robs her of intimacy with her Beloved; robs her of intimacy that empowers her to run.

VERSE 12

Before I was even aware,

My soul had made me

As the chariots of my noble people.

The maiden had been working in her Beloved's interests in the previous verse when suddenly she was drawn into the King's presence. The text even reads as if she were "transported in the spirit." He and His friends are calling to her to return to Him to dance before him. Could the maiden be seeing a vision of the **rapture** as recorded in Thessalonians?

> **I Thess. 4:16-17 For the Lord Himself will descend from heaven with a shout, with the voice of an archangel, and with the trumpet of God. And**

---

[6] Merriam Webster's collegiate dictionary, 10th edition

the dead in Christ will rise first. Then we who are alive and remain shall be caught up together with them in the clouds to meet the Lord in the air. And thus we shall always be with the Lord. (NKJV)

Are her noble people those referred to as the "dead in Christ" who will rise first that are mentioned in this scripture? The first vision of the Song came while the maiden was embracing the King. This vision, the second vision of the Song comes to her while she is working in the King's interests. We can see a clear picture of the "drawing" and the "running" in the two visions.

Matt. 24:45-46 "Who then is a faithful and wise servant, whom his master made ruler over his household, to give them food in due season? Blessed is that servant whom his master, when he comes, will find so doing." (NKJV)

After the contract was sealed, in the Jewish tradition of marriage, the bridegroom would go back to his father's house and he would prepare a place to bring his bride to live. Many times it would be a room in his father's house. When the dwelling place was ready and the bridegroom's father gave his approval, the bridegroom would gather his friends and they would surprise the bride, who was prepared and waiting, with a shout after they were within hearing distance. He would then quickly steal her away into the night to carry her to the wedding festivities and to the place that he had prepared for them.

John 14:2-3 "In My Father's house are many mansions; if it were not so, I would have told you. I go to prepare a place for you. And if I go and prepare a place for you, I will come again and receive you to Myself, that where I am, there you may be also." (NKJV)

These things speak to me of the rapture when Jesus, the great Bridegroom, will suddenly come and steal His bride away.

In the next verse, could the dance to which the King is calling her be a description of the beginning of the culmination of the ages and the end of time as we know it?

I Pet. 4:7 But the end of all things is at hand; therefore be serious and watchful in your prayers. (NKJV)

Is the King's description of the maiden as she dances in the next chapter a picture of the gloriously spotless and blameless bride that Jesus will present to Himself one day; a bride-queen who is prepared and ready to fulfill her destiny and take her place in the Kingdom to rule and reign with Him at His side?

Eph. 5:27 ...that he might present her to Himself a glorious church, not having spot or wrinkle or any such thing, but that she should be holy and without blemish. (NKJV)

Child of God, if this be so, and you have determined to have the Prize, then you would do well to study the journey of the maiden in this song! I encourage you to learn from her experience. It is no coincidence that this lovely book is in God's Word, for I believe that it holds a vital message for the church of today – the church of the last days before the return of Jesus.

VERSE 13

THE BELOVED AND HIS FRIENDS

Return, return, O Shulamite;

Return, return, that we may look upon you!

THE SHULAMITE

What would you see in the Shulamite –

As it were, the dance of the two camps?

- *His friends refers symbolically to the groom's party.*

In this vision the maiden sees a scene at the wedding of the Bridegroom and His bride. The Beloved has joined His groom's party and they are calling for the wedding dance, the dance of the two camps. This dance is also called the dance of *Mahanaim*. I am always inspired when I see worship to my King expressed in the dance. I love that form of worship. Well, this book that Solomon has written is the "Song of Songs" and this dance is the **dance of all dances.**

The Bridegroom King and His friends watch with great joy and celebration as the glorious Shulamite maiden dances the victorious wedding dance. Here we see Jew and Gentile, Israel (referred to in Hosea as God's wife) and the church all coming together in God's Kingdom as one family in Him.

> **Eph. 2:14-15 For He Himself is our peace, who has made both (Jew and Gentile) one, and has broken down the middle wall of separation, having abolished in His flesh the enmity, that is, the law of commandments contained in ordinances, so as to create in Himself one new man from the two, thus making peace. (NKJV)**

I believe that in the previous verse, as the maiden was working in the King's interests, she saw a vision of the rapture. In this verse, I believe she is seeing a vision of what will transpire in the life of Israel and the church prior to the rapture, and how it will appear in the Kingdom.

What she is seeing, in this vision of the dance, is a prophetic picture of an event that Satan has fought to prevent down through the ages of time. However, it is an event that God has purposed to come to pass. We see here the two camps. These are God's major interests first spoken of in chapter two, verse thirteen. They are the church (Jew and Gentile) and Israel. In this vision they are strong, being united in love and purpose, and together, victorious over Satan and his efforts to divide them.

> **Eph. 3:14-15 For this reason I bow my knees to the Father of our Lord Jesus Christ, from whom the whole family in heaven and earth is named... (NKJV)**

I Cor. 2:9-10 But as it is written:

"Eye has not seen, nor ear heard,
Nor have entered into the heart of man
The things which God has prepared for those who love him."

But God has revealed them to us through His Spirit. For the Spirit
searches all things, yes, the deep things of God. (NKJV)

Isa. 54:5 For your Maker is your husband,
The Lord of hosts is His name;
And your Redeemer is the Holy One of Israel;
He is called the God of the whole earth. (NKJV)

Understanding this "dance of all dances" is like putting a puzzle together and the information I am laying out for you are the pieces to the puzzle.

In the NKJV which I use, this dance is referred to as the "dance of two camps." In the footnotes, the Hebrew name of the dance is given as **"Mahanaim** (ma kha na' im, transliterated).

Mahanaim is a place first mentioned in Genesis 32:2 which is also referred to as God's camp and it was a Levitical city in Solomon's day. The translated English word of camps can be rendered several different ways according to different sources. All of these renditions are pertinent in understanding the content of this verse. Contextually, in the story of Jacob, it could refer to **armies** or as **lines.**

Mahanaim as mentioned in the story of Jacob, whose story begins in the 28th chapter of Genesis, is a place where the angels of God met with Jacob. It is a place where Heaven and earth met, and could possibly be known as "the camp of angels and men."

Another possible explanation of the meaning of Mahanaim as used in Solomon's song, when the dance is referred to as "the dance of two camps," could be speaking of Jacob's actual company or entourage. In this story, as they were returning to his home, the two companies were made up of Leah and her camp and Rachel and her camp.

Leah, the older sister, was the father's choice. Leah and her camp are symbolic of Israel, referred to in scripture as God's wife and as the chosen of God, the Father. Rachel, the Bridegroom's choice, and her camp are symbolic of the church and Jesus' chosen bride, made up of Jew and Gentile.

"The New Living Bible" renders the last portion of verse 13 this way:

*"Why do you gaze so intently at this young woman of Shulam as she moves so gracefully **between** two lines of dancers?"*

In the dance of Mahanaim, I believe that one line of dancers is like Leah and her camp, and represent Israel, God's chosen, which is spoken of as God's wife in scripture. The other line of dancers is like Rachel and her camp and represents the church (Jew and Gentile). They are Jesus' chosen.

- ***Shulamite means daughter of peace and is the feminine form of***
  Solomon which also means peace.

These are the puzzle pieces. Now let's put them together!

In this vision the maiden has become an instrument of peace as she dances between the two lines of dancers. She has been instrumental in reconciling Jew and Gentile, the church and Israel, and the church and Israel to God. She is giving us a picture of the priesthood, and this is a dance of peace as Jew and Gentile come together. This is the place where, in unity, oneness, harmony, and fellowship, God's life flows from camp to camp in the blessed family of the Kingdom of God.

It is a great celebration for they have all defeated the enemy of their soul, the devil. The word, devil, literally means to divide without a cause.

I believe that this verse in the song is a glorious prophetic picture of the passionate and victorious warrior bride, and the two camps or armies that are mentioned here, the Gentile camp and the Jewish camp, have come together to make up the glorious church of the last days.

It is a picture of the mature bride of Christ dancing the bridal dance of peace, as she moves gracefully between the two camps or companies, uniting the two, Jew and Gentile, Israel and the church. That this wall of division comes down between the two should be a matter of great concern to the church of today! This is huge because I believe that what we are seeing here is the last great move of God before the return of Jesus!

As we look back at the description of the Shulamite maiden in the beginning of the song and compare that description to the way she is described here in chapter six, we see that this is a dance that testifies of God's transforming, overcoming power. It encourages and inspires the people of God to press on – to relentlessly pursue their call to become all that He has purposed for them in His Kingdom.

Now this dance is also referred to as the dance of God's camp, and I believe He is present in this vision to receive His wife, Israel, who has returned to Him. She has returned to her Beloved Ishi (a Hebrew word meaning husband), from her wanderings and her harlotries. This "dance of God's camp" is a picture of the fulfillment of the words of the prophet, Hosea.

Hos. 2:19-20 I will betroth you to Me forever;
Yes, I will betroth you to Me
In righteousness and mercy;
In lovingkindness and mercy;
I will betroth you to Me in faithfulness,
And you shall know the Lord. (NKJV)

And God is present to celebrate His Son's bride-queen!

Is it any wonder, then, that we find the Holy Spirit instructing and teaching us, the Gentile camp, about our Bridegroom's Hebrew traditions, since we will undoubtedly be a very integral part of them one day soon?

The Word tells us that we will celebrate, for instance, the Feast of Tabernacles in the Kingdom of God. Learning these Hebrew traditions, I believe, is a part of our preparation in order for us to be able to take our place in His Kingdom as the bride-queen of Christ.

Zech. 14:16 And it shall come to pass that everyone who is left of all the nations which came against Jerusalem shall go up from year to year to worship the King, the Lord of hosts, and to keep the Feast of Tabernacles. (NKJV)

Lev. 23:41 You shall keep it as a feast to the Lord for seven days in the year. It shall be a statute forever in your generations. You shall celebrate it in the seventh month. (NKJV)

The church, for the most part, has viewed the feasts as Jewish feasts down through the ages, but these feasts are not just Jewish feasts. They are God's feasts, and it is plain to me from these scriptures above that He has meant all along for the church (Jew and Gentile) to enjoy them, especially the Feast of Tabernacles.

Saints of God, look for the church to embrace more of an understanding of Jewish tradition in these last days. The church must strive to reach out to the Jewish people to bring to them the peace that is afforded by knowing Jesus.

You will note that in the illustration of the King on His wedding day, the day of the gladness of His heart in chapter three, I have pictured Him wearing a talit or prayer shawl which I will cover more thoroughly in chapter eight. In Jewish tradition, the bride presents a talit to her groom on their wedding day. He wears the talit which is to say, "I will be true to my wife and to my God!" It symbolizes his fidelity. She, in giving, him the talit, is saying, "I give my heart and love to you!"

When she embraces her Jewish roots, the bride of Christ is symbolically placing the talit on her Bridegroom and restoring His original Jewishness.

I believe that the seal which the maiden asks her Beloved to place on His arm and on his heart is represented by the talit. We will learn more about that in verse six of chapter eight.

In my illustration of the Shulamite maiden as the Bridegroom describes her in chapter seven, I portray her holding the talit as she dances. The talit, I believe, is also representative of the Prize to which she has finally laid hold. You will remember that the Prize is the bridal love that the King and His bride share for one another. In chapter eight of the song, she will lay it at His feet, as she asks if she can place it over His heart and arm.

In 2005, when I saw the Shulamite maiden in my spirit, as described in chapter six of the song, she was dancing with what I thought was a robe or cloak. I drew her as I saw her even though I didn't understand why she was dancing with a robe... it just seemed correct. Two years later, the Holy Spirit revealed to me that it is a talit that the maiden in my illustration is holding.

Recently, I was leading praise and worship at a celebration of the Feast of Tabernacles with a group of Gentile and Messianic Jewish believers. A Jewish man and his lovely wife danced together in joyful, childlike abandon before the Lord with his talit. Later, as I reflected on this lovely expression of worship, I was reminded of the maiden in the song and her passionate wedding dance before the King. I just wouldn't be surprised, when the glorious event takes place if our Bridegroom, Jesus, doesn't join His bride-queen in joyful dancing in like manner!

Zeph. 3:17 The Lord your God is with you, He is mighty to save. He will take great delight in you, He will quiet you with His love, He will rejoice over you with singing. (NIV)

CHAPTER SIX REVIEW

1. To where did the Shulamite tell the daughters of Jerusalem her Beloved had gone? __

_____

2. What must the maiden do to find her Beloved again? _____

_____

3. How does "a lily among thorns" describe the Shulamite maiden? _____

_____

4. In the context of this song, who are the queens? _____

_____

5. In the context of this song who are the concubines? _____

_____

6. Who is being described as "fair as the moon, clear as the sun?" _____

_____

7. What kind of people are found in the "garden of nuts"? _____

_____

8. "The garden of nuts" is in a valley. What does the valley symbolize? _____

_____

9. To what does the "dance of the two camps" refer? _____

_____

10. What is the maiden holding when she does the "dance of the two camps"? _____

_____

CHAPTER SEVEN

THE DANCE

VERSE 1

THE BELOVED

How beautiful are your feet in sandals,

O prince's daughter!

The curves of your thighs are like jewels,

The work of the hands of a skillful workman.

- *Skillful workman is the Holy Spirit.*

The Beloved Bridegroom King begins to describe His glorious, mature bride in the vision as she dances before Him and His friends. This is a description of the bride of Christ and her ministry in the last days before Jesus returns.

The King is confirming her ministry with His remarks in the first three verses of this chapter. In this verse, He praises her ability to bring the good news of the Gospel. This is evangelism as she functions in the priesthood reconciling man to God.

> **Eph. 6:15 ...and having shod your feet with the preparation of the gospel of peace. (NKJV)**

> **Isa. 52:7 How beautiful upon the mountains**
> **Are the feet of him who brings good news,**
> **Who proclaims peace,**
> **Who brings glad tidings of good things,**
> **Who proclaims salvation,**
> **Who says to Zion,**
> **"Your God reigns." (NKJV)**

The King calls the maiden a prince's daughter because she has been born again into a royal lineage and a royal priesthood.

- *"Curves of your thighs" speaks of strength.*

- *Jewels are symbolic of wisdom.*

- *The "work of the hands of a skillful workman" is speaking of the Holy Spirit and His transforming work that has taken place in her life.*

The King admires the strength of her wisdom that has come from the Holy Spirit and His work in her life – a work that has transformed this humble shepherd girl into His glorious, victorious bride, a royal daughter in the family of God who is ready to take her place in His Father's Kingdom.

> **Psa. 45:13-15 The royal daughter is all glorious within the palace;**
> **Her clothing is woven with gold.**
> **She shall be brought to the King in robes of many colors,**
> **The virgins, her companions who follow her, shall be brought to You.**
> **With gladness and rejoicing they shall be brought;**
> **They shall enter the King's palace.**

VERSE 2

Your navel is a rounded goblet;

It lacks no blended beverage.

Your waist is a heap of wheat

Set about with lilies.

- *Navel speaks of one's ability to receive nurturing.*

- *Rounded speaks of abundance.*

- *Goblet is a vessel for wine, and wine is symbolic of the joy of the Holy Spirit at work in you.*

- *Blended speaks of a good combination.*

- *Waist represents the place of one's spirit.*

John 7:38 "...out of his belly shall flow rivers of living waters."
7:39 But this he spoke of the Spirit... (KJV)

- *Wheat is the bread of life referring to the Word.*

- *Lilies is symbolic of the bride-queen of Christ.*

This glorious bride is a vessel that receives and carries an abundant and continual infilling of a perfect blend of Holy Spirit revealed (rhema) Word into her life. She is pregnant with **rhema** Word that she has received and meditated on while in the secret places with the King. That word has produced life in her, and she will carry it in her spirit until it comes forth in ministry. That rhema word is affirmed and supported by the bride company and it pours forth out of her spirit in ministry to those whom the King has prepared to receive it.

VERSE 3

Your two breasts are like two fawns,

Twins of a gazelle.

- *Breasts are symbolic of the ability to nurture.*

- *Two speaks of the two testaments.*

- *Fawns are symbolic of young Christians in or near their mother, the does of the field.*

- *Twins speaks of balance.*

- *Gazelle is symbolic of the resurrected Jesus.*

The King is affirming the maiden's ability to nurture the Christians who will become a part of the bride company with a balance of the Word from both the Old Testament and the New Testament of the resurrected Jesus.

This is discipleship!

> **Matt. 13:52 Then He spoke to them, Therefore every scribe instructed concerning the kingdom of heaven is like a householder who brings out of his treasure things both new and old." (scribe is a scholar of the Old Testament) (NKJV)**

VERSE 4

Your neck is like an ivory tower,

Your eyes like the pools in Heshbon

By the gate of Bath Rabbim.

Your nose is like the tower of Lebanon

Which looks toward Damascus.

In these next two verses the Beloved is praising the maiden's Godly virtues to rule with Him.

- *Neck is symbolic of one's will.*
- *Ivory is the substance that kings' thrones were made of. It is symbolic of royalty.*

- *Tower was a lookout or vantage point to keep watch against the approaching enemy.*

- *Eyes speak of one's insight.*

- *Pools speaks of clearness as in clear water.*

- *Heshbon means fertile.*

- *Gate symbolizes access to one's mind.*

- *Bath Rabbim means the promise of many.*

- *Nose is symbolic of discernment.*

- *Lebanon speaks of the glory and majesty of God. It literally means white or white mountain.*

- *Damascus speaks of one's enemy.*

The maiden's will to rule and reign with Him is demonstrated by a royal strength of character that desires to protect her people from their enemies. She has clear insight into spiritual matters that enter and influence the fertile minds of the many people that she will help to govern.

The King sees that she has discernment in protecting her people from the approaching enemy. This discernment has come from the time she has spent in the presence of the glory and majesty of God and it has made her a formidable foe to the enemy. She is a mighty royal warrior in battle against the enemy of her people. **She is an intercessor,** and like Jesus, our great high priest, who always loves to make intercession for us.

> **Heb. 7:26 For such a high priest was fitting for us, who is holy, harmless, undefiled, separate from sinners, and has become higher than the heavens. (NKJV)**

VERSE 5

Your head crowns you like Mount Carmel,

And the hair of your head is like purple;

A king is held captive by your tresses.

- *Head is symbolic of leadership.*

Mount Carmel is a beautiful mountain overlooking the Mediterranean Sea which rises above the lovely city of Haifa in Israel. It is the place where Elijah faced and defeated the prophets of Baal.

- *Hair is symbolic of separation unto God.*

- *Purple is symbolic of royalty.*

The maiden's total submission to her Beloved (her head) graces her life with the boldness to confront and defeat the enemy and qualifies her to be a Godly leader. Her separation and consecration unto God is with the kind of royal elegance and grace that captures and holds the admiration and attention of the King.

VERSE 6

How fair and how pleasant you are,

O love, with your delights.

- *Fair means beautiful and unveiled.*

The maiden is dancing before the King unveiled and he exclaims that she is beautiful to Him in her transparent and vulnerable state. The maiden is not only transparent and vulnerable to Him, but to all others who are present at the wedding festivities as well. He calls her His love and expresses to all present His delight in her.

In chapter four, this maiden ravished the King's heart with her ability to stay focused on Him as she learned spiritual warfare. He was overcome with her in chapter six when she kept her eyes on Him as she walked through her dark hour of chastisement. She captivated Him in the previous verse because of her consecration to God with such royal elegance.

Now this formidable warrior pleasantly delights Him with the beauty of transparency and vulnerability that she displays to all present in her dance of peace. These words do not seem to fit in the same sentence. Here is another paradox – this maiden is like velvet steel!

VERSE 7

This stature of yours is like a palm tree,

And your breasts like its clusters.

- *Stature refers to spiritual maturity.*

The King is comparing the maiden's spiritual maturity to that of a palm tree. A palm tree is a symbol of beauty and prosperity.

It is always green (lush with life), and its roots go deep to keep it grounded in a storm. It is flexible to bend in strong winds so that it doesn't snap and break. They are stronger in groups. They thrive under pressure. They grow in pure soil. Because their roots go deep, they are well watered even in the dry seasons. The date clusters of the date palm which are common in Israel are very sweet and nutritious.

- *Breasts are symbolic of one's ability to nurture.*

- *In this context, clusters are the fruit of the palm tree.*

The King is saying that the maiden is a witness to everyone around her all year long with the lushness of His life flowing through her; that she is so grounded in His love for her that she will endure all of the storms of life; she will not snap and break when the harsh winds of adversity come against her but she will bend with them.

He admires her ability to function and grow strong in the place where she has been placed within the body of Christ. She has the ability to thrive there where the soil is pure under the pressures of life. He sees her ability to draw sustenance from God's love during the hard, dry seasons of her life, and He admires the sweet, nutritious fruitfulness that He sees in her spiritual walk.

VERSE 8

I said, "I will go up to the palm tree,

I will take hold of its branches."

Let now your breasts be like the clusters of the vine,

The fragrance of your breath like apples.

I like what Mike Bickle says about this verse and I quote, "Jesus is saying, 'I will release the manifested power of My presence in My mature bride. I will take hold of her branches (ministries) and there will be revival in the church through the mature bride unprecedented in the last days.'"[7]

The next part of this verse and the first part of verse nine are three prophetic commissions to the bride of Christ from the King.

---

[7] "Song of Songs" by Mike Bickle

1. The King is commissioning the bride to nurture and refresh the church with the fruits of her spiritual maturity through example or through her very lifestyle. She is real! She lives what she teaches!

- *Vine is symbolic of the church.*

- *Breath is symbolic of one's inner life or spirit.*

- *Apples are symbolic of the revelation truth from the Word by the Holy Spirit (rhema word).*

- *Fragrance is symbolic of "the evidence."*

2. The King is commissioning her to bring forth and minister to the church the rhema Word that she has received and carried in her spirit until now. It is evident to the church that her teaching comes from the anointing of the Holy Spirit at work in her life.

VERSE 9

And the roof of your mouth like the best wine.

3. The third commission from the King is that every word this maiden speaks will be inspired and powerfully anointed by the Holy Spirit.

THE SHULAMITE

The wine goes down smoothly for my beloved,

Moving gently the lips of sleepers.

The second vision ends. The maiden has received joyfully the work of the Holy Spirit into her life with no resistance, which continues to enhance the intimacy that she enjoys with her Beloved. The relationship that she enjoys with Him gently arouses others around her from their spiritual lethargy to begin to ask for His kisses.

VERSE 10

I am my beloved's,

And his desire is toward me.

The vision has ended and the maiden makes this passionate proclamation!

Note the progression in the maiden's remarks about her relationship with her Beloved King:

"...My Beloved is to me..." She is focused on what she has in Jesus.
(Chapter 1, verse 13-14)

"My Beloved is mine and I am his." She is still focused on her benefits in this relationship first, but is now starting to realize that she belongs to Him.
(Chapter 2, verse 16)

"I am my beloved's and he is mine." Her priorities are changing from concern for what she is receiving in this relationship to what she is to Him. She is showing more concern for His needs that for her own.
(Chapter 6, verse 13)

The maiden is now totally focused on her Beloved and His desires in this verse. This selfless attitude has developed in her as her greatest need, the need to feel valued, is met in Jesus. This attitude of selflessness has matured through the fullness of testing. She is now empowered to unconditionally love her King as well as others, as we will so clearly see in the next verses.

As the maiden has matured through her pursuit of the King's bridal love for His bride, (the Prize), her love for the King has evolved from a **selfish** love into a **selfless** love and she is able to return that same bridal love back to Him. That selfless, agape love for the King overflows from her life to others. Agape is a Greek word meaning the God kind of self-sacrificial love.

The King has continuously poured agape love into the maiden's life throughout the song and that love has transformed her. She is now a bride-queen, His lily, who moves with grace and confidence toward her destiny in the Kingdom and to the Prize!

I am my Beloveds and
His desire is toward me.
Song of Solomon 7:10

Karyl Simmons '06'

VERSE 11

Come my beloved,

Let us go into the field;

Let us lodge in the villages.

- *The field is the world of unsaved, lost souls where the body of Christ goes outside of the church to evangelize.*

Matt. 13:38 "The field is the world..." (NKJV)

- *Villages is symbolic of the daughters of Jerusalem worldwide; both Jew and Gentile.*

This verse gives us insight into the maiden's attitude toward ministry. There is no hesitancy here to run with her Beloved as there was in chapter five. In fact, she is eagerly initiating ministry now. She is also asking to spend intimate time with Him among the daughters of Jerusalem, world wide, as they work together in the fields that are white unto harvest. We see here the balance of drawing in intimacy and running in ministry once again.

The bride company worldwide is composed of Jew and Gentile Christians operating as one together, with no barriers between them. We will see in the next verse that the King does not mention the fig tree, which is symbolic of Israel, when He is talking about His vineyard. Both are His areas of interest as we saw in verse 13 of chapter 2. You will remember, in the vision of the last verse of chapter 6, that we saw Israel and the church, (referred to as the grape vine), united as one family in the dance of Mahanaim. I believe, at this point in the song, that this vision has come to pass and that they are now together and functioning as the priesthood in the church. This is why the fig tree is not mentioned as one of the King's interests in the next verse.

VERSE 12

Let us get up early to the vineyards;

Let us see if the vine has budded,

Whether the grape blossoms are open,

And the pomegranates are in bloom.

There I will give you my love.

- *Vineyards are one's interests*

- *Vine symbolizes the church.*

- *Grape blossoms are the promise of new Christians in the church.*

- *Pomegranates symbolize the priesthood.*

We see here that the maiden's interests have become the King's interests, and now the King's interests are the church and the priesthood. The maiden is excited to rise up <u>early</u> to check on the progress in the church of promising new Christians and she is eager to encourage the maturing Christians who are ready to enter the priesthood of believers as she offers the King her love.

Again we see that the maiden is initiating a perfect balance of running in ministry and of drawing apart for intimacy.

VERSE 13

The mandrakes give off a fragrance,

And at our gates are pleasant fruits

All manner, new and old,

Which I have laid up for you, my beloved.

- *A mandrake is a purple flower with a lovely fragrance known in the ancient world as a love fruit. It speaks of intimacy.*

- *Fragrance is the evidence of.*

- *Gates represent access to one's mind.*

The intimate relationship the King and the maiden have with one another is evident to all those around them. This special relationship opens up everyone's mind to the possibility of having intimacy in their own lives with the King which would produce the kind of fruit that they see in the maiden's life. There is new fruit being produced in her life on a continual basis and there is old fruit that remains – fruit that honors the King.

> **John 15:16 "You did not choose Me, but I chose you and appointed you that you should go and bear fruit, and that your fruit should remain, ..." (NKJV)**

> **Matt. 13:59 He said to them, "Therefore every teacher of the law who has been instructed about the kingdom of heaven is like the owner of a**

house who brings out of his storeroom new treasures as well as old." (NIV)

CHAPTER SEVEN REVIEW

1. "The work of a skillful worker" speaks of what? _____

_____

2. The maiden's waist being described as a "heap of wheat" means what? _____

_____

3. In the context of this study, what is discipleship? _____

_____

4. The maiden's nose looking toward Damascus means what? _____

_____

5. How can the maiden be described as "velvet steel"? _____

_____

6. What does a palm tree symbolize? _____

7. The church is symbolized by _____

_____

8. What are the three commissions given to the maiden by the King? _____

_____

9. Where is the "field"? _____

_____

10. What is a mandrake and of what does it speak? _____

_____

CHAPTER EIGHT

THE GLORIOUS BRIDE-QUEEN

VERSE 1

Oh, that you were like my brother,

Who nursed at my mother's breasts!

If I should find you outside,

I would kiss you;

I would not be despised.

The next two verses give us insight into the nature of the mature bride's attitude toward the church. The Shulamite maiden laments the fact that she could embrace her brothers' instruction and discipline within the church and not be despised, which was her condition before she asked the King to draw her. Her brothers were nurtured in the church just as she was, but they did not know her Beloved.

> **Matt. 7:21-23 "Not everyone who says to Me, 'Lord, Lord,' shall enter the kingdom of heaven, but he who does the will of My Father in heaven.**
> **"Many will say to Me in that day, 'Lord, Lord, have we not prophesized in Your name and done many wonders in Your name?'**
> **"And then I will declare to them, 'I never knew you; depart from Me, you who practice lawlessness!' (NKJV)**

> **Luke 13:22-27 And He went through the cities and villages, teaching, and journeying toward Jerusalem.**
> **Then one said to Him, "Lord, are there few who are saved?" And He said to them,**
> **"Strive to enter through the narrow gate, for many, I say to you, will seek to enter and will not be able.**
> **"When once the Master of the house has risen up and shut the door, and you begin to stand outside and knock at the door, saying, "Lord, Lord, open for us, and He will answer and say to you, 'I do not know you, where you are from,"**
> **"then you will begin to say, 'We ate and drank in Your presence, and You taught in our streets.'**
> **"But He will say, 'I tell you I do not know you, where you are from. Depart from Me, all you workers of iniquity.'**

The word, **know**, is the same word used in the following passage found in Matthew.

Matt. 1:24-25 Then Joseph, being aroused from sleep, did as the angel of the Lord commanded him and took to him his wife. and did not know her till she had brought forth her firstborn Son. And he called His name Jesus.

This kind of knowing speaks to me of the drawing aside to spend intimate time with the King, meditating on His word and coming to know Him in a richer, more meaningful relationship. It speaks of bearing the fruit that this kind of intimate relationship creates in one's life.

The maiden longs to see her brothers and others in her church family find the richness of knowing her Beloved like she has come to know Him and the transformation that knowing Him has brought into her life. There will be a dramatic transformation in the life of one who comes to know the Lord intimately.

This verse gives us insight into the maiden's heart, in her ability to graciously forgive those who have wronged her in the church.

Can we do any less? Having asked this question, I must point out that this scripture suggests to me that the church at large, for the most part at this point in time, will be strongly influenced by the brothers' mentality. Their legalistic approach to the word and their lack of an intimate relationship with the Bridegroom King pose quite a challenge for the bride of Christ.

Saints of God, we must understand that the church is not perfect. As I've said before, and I reiterate here, it is made up of imperfect people like you and me. But the church is God's idea and it is a part of God's plan for our lives. The church, as imperfect as it is, serves God's purposes and He uses it effectively to mature us in our Christian walk. It has been my observation over the years that "lone rangers" do not fare well in God's kingdom! And God requires us to work alongside of our church family and faithfully serve Him in our churches as He directs.

VERSE 2

I would lead you and bring you

Into the house of my mother,

She who used to instruct me.

I would cause you to drink of spiced wine,

Of the juice of my pomegranate.

- *Spice is symbolic of the various administrations of the Holy Spirit at work in one's life.*

- *Wine is symbolic of the joy of the Holy Spirit at work in one's life.*

- *Juice of her pomegranate speaks of the results of her priestly administrations to others.*

When the maiden says, "I would lead you..." it suggests to me that this maiden, who was instructed to follow the King and His shepherds in the beginning of this song, has now matured to a place in her journey where she, like John the Baptist, is able to prepare the way of the Lord to make His paths straight. **(Mark 1:2-4)**

Again we see here her heart for the church! She is saying, "If it were possible, I would present my Beloved to the church in such a way as to give every single person there in the life of the church an opportunity to know Him intimately." She longs for all in her church family to have the same life-changing relationship that she enjoys with her Beloved King; to know what it is to draw apart for intimacy with Him and what it is to run with Him in effective ministry. But it is a hard place in which to be sometimes when the student becomes the teacher.

The student has become a powerfully anointed teacher and those in the church who were effective in teaching the maiden the things of God as a young Christian could benefit from the things she has learned as well.

Heb. 5:12 For though by this time you ought to be teachers... (NKJV)

She longs to see her Beloved blessed by the joy of the Holy Spirit's various administrations at work in the lives of all those in the life of the church and by the nurturing effects of her priestly administrations to them in her efforts to reconcile them to God and to one another.

She wishes that life in this fallen world was such that she would not have to hold back on anything. But she understands that the King's kisses cannot be fully expressed in a public setting where there are those who are not yet ready to accept them.

This maiden is just bursting with love for her King. She finds it difficult to hold back her emotions. However, in this situation, her restraint reveals a great amount of character, humility, and wisdom. Perhaps her attempts in chapter three, verse four were unfruitful. At any rate, this maiden has learned to run in ministry only when the Beloved urges her to do so.

So many times in my own walk, I have run ahead of the Lord in my eagerness to serve, and failed to wait for the Lord's unction and God's perfect timing. These vain attempts have only proven to be unfruitful and a waste of time and energy that could have been put to better use elsewhere.

Isa. 40:31 But those who wait on the Lord shall renew their strength;
They shall mount up with wings like eagles,
They shall run and not be weary,
They shall walk and not faint. (NKJV)

VERSE 3

(TO THE DAUGHTERS OF JERUSAALEM)

His left hand is under my head,

And his right hand embraces me.

The maiden turns to the bride company and shares her joy with them in the fact that she is back in the King's embrace. Once again, she is in that place where her mind is being renewed and where the affections of her heart are being even more firmly fixed on Him. This is the time to lay those troublesome concerns about her church family at His feet and just soak in His love.

Christian, we must learn to trust God's timing and His ways for those we love and who do not see the need yet for a deeper walk like the one you may be enjoying. We must respect their freedom of choice and we must obey the Lord in what He instructs us to do concerning them. When we've done that, then we must let go of them and just rest in the King's embrace.

VERSE 4

I charge you, O daughters of Jerusalem,

Do not stir up nor awaken love

Until it pleases.

The maiden is now with like minded people in the bride company as she enjoys the King's embrace. She asks them not to disturb her and her Beloved, nor to disrupt their time together. Once again, she encourages the bride company to resist the temptation to rush others prematurely into the King's embrace before they are ready.

VERSE 5

A RELATIVE

Who is this coming up from the wilderness,

Leaning upon her beloved?

I awakened you under the apple tree.

There your mother brought you forth;

There she who bore you brought you forth.

The scene has changed again and I believe that this verse is describing another prophetic dream or vision that the maiden sees while in the King's embrace. It is the third vision of the song and it is electric with emotions. It is giving you and me a picture of "that day" in the Kingdom. It is that moment in time where all of mankind down through the ages watch as Jesus reveals His bride-queen and presents her to His Father. It is a scene that is taking place in the Kingdom of Heaven at the consummation of the ages. The Bridegroom and His glorious bride are coming up from the wilderness. You will note that in chapter three, verse six, they were coming out from the wilderness. But this verse, "coming up" speaks to me of the end of this present world as we know it and of entering the Kingdom of Heaven. What a promotion!

- *The relative is another character in the song. This is someone in her church family.*

- *Coming up speaks of promotion.*

- *Wilderness is symbolic of our wandering through the world as we depend on God alone to provide.*

- *Apple tree speaks of Jesus.*

- *Her mother is the church.*

In this vision, a part of her church family sees the Shulamite maiden "coming up," which is "to be promoted" from her wandering in the world on her life's journey, totally dependent upon her Beloved King and His provision. She is moving into the Kingdom of Heaven and to her destiny as the King's bride-queen; that glorious impossibility has come to pass! There has been such a transformation in her and she is now so much like her Beloved that the relative is not able to recognize her at first.

I believe that the maiden is now seeing herself in her glorified, resurrected body. Just as Jesus' friends did not immediately recognize Him after His resurrection, the bride's relative does not recognize her. The sanctifying work of the Holy Spirit has been completed in her, and she is seeing what that looks like in this vision.

Rom. 8:22-23 For we know that the whole creation groans and labors with birth pangs together until now.
Not only that, but we who have the firstfruits of the Spirit, even we ourselves groan within ourselves, eagerly waiting for the adoption, the redemption of our body. (NKJV)
Rom. 8:29-30 For whom He forknew, He also predestined to be conformed to the image of His Son, that He might be the firstborn among many brethren.
Moreover whom He predestined, these He also called; whom He called, these He also justified; and whom He justified, these He also glorified. (NKJV)

You can read in I Corinthians 15:35-49 to learn more about our glorified bodies. In the Gospel of John, chapters 20 and 21, you will find a vivid description of Jesus in His glorified body. The dark, ordinary shepherdess of chapter one has now entered the ranks of the daughters of Zion first mentioned in chapter three.

Suddenly, the relative realizes who the maiden is and remembers teaching her spiritual truths about Jesus when she was a young shepherd girl in the church. The church is where she was introduced to Jesus, the Bridegroom King, and where she sealed the contract of marriage with Him. It is where she was born again and where her transformation began to take place.

VERSE 6

THE SHULAMITE TO HER BELOVED

Set me as a seal upon your heart,

As a seal upon your arm;

For love is as strong as death,

Jealousy as cruel as the grave;

Its flames are flames of fire,

A most vehement flame.

We are a spirit that has a soul and lives in a body!

The maiden's body was sealed for the King alone when she accepted the veil in verse 7 of chapter 1. The maiden's **soul** was sealed with the Holy Spirit of promise, her guarantee that her Beloved would return for her when she accepted the cup of wine. This wine was mentioned in chapter 1 and represents the joy of the Holy Spirit at work in her.

> **Eph. 1:13-14 In Him you also trusted, after you heard the word of truth, the gospel of your salvation; in whom also, having believed, you were sealed with the Holy Spirit of promise,**
> **Who is the guarantee of our inheritance until the redemption of the purchased possession, to the praise of His glory. (NKJV)**

Then the maiden became a **fountain sealed** in chapter 4 when her spirit was sealed for her Beloved alone.

We are a spirit that has a soul and lives in a body. We are being sanctified completely so that our whole spirit, soul, and body will be preserved and blameless at the coming of our Lord Jesus Christ.

> **I Thess. 5:23 Now may the God of peace Himself sanctify you completely, and may your whole spirit, soul, and body be preserved blameless at the coming of our Lord Jesus Christ. (NKJV)**

In this verse, we see the maiden asking her Beloved to set her as a **seal** on His heart and on His arm by accepting her bridal love for Him...the Prize.

Until this point, the Beloved Bridegroom has been gathering lilies (those in the bride company who finally move on to become the King's bride-queen). Now the time of gathering lilies is over and the bride is ready to take her place in the Kingdom.

This seal is like a personal signature that permanently identifies the Bridegroom as belonging forever to His bride and her to Him. The wedding rings that a bride and groom exchange today carry this idea.

I believe that this seal is symbolic of the Prize and is represented by the talit. The talit is symbolic of their bridal love for one another. In Jewish tradition, the bride presented a talit to her groom on their wedding day. In wearing the talit, he was saying, "I will be true to my wife and to my God." It symbolized his fidelity. She, in giving him the talit, was saying, "I give my heart and love to you."

In this vision, the maiden sees that she has finally laid hold of the Prize. She is able to love Him in the same way that He loves her. This love she holds for her Beloved has matured through the fullness of testing, and she lays the Prize at His feet! She is asking Him to wear the talit as a seal and a symbol of the Prize to which she has laid hold. Because of this shared bridal love for one another, our Shulamite maiden is asking her Beloved Bridegroom King to make her His bride-queen.

The talit is a four cornered shawl with fringes and tassels on each corner. It is a garment or mantle of glory and honor. When a Jewish man wears it, it protects him from worldly influences and under it he has intimacy with the Lord and he feels a sense of God's unconditional love and nearness. There is a band or border along one side of the shawl. This is called the crown and this is the side that is placed over the head and around the face when he prays. It is like his prayer closet. Every part of the talit has symbolic meaning to the Jew.

In the illustration of the King on His wedding day (the day of the gladness of His heart in chapter three), I have pictured Him wearing a talit. This is the talit as shown in the illustration in chapter six, which the maiden holds in the dance of all dances.

The Shulamite begins to give us a description of this bridal love in this verse. She tells us that this bridal love is stronger than death. It was this love that sent Jesus to and kept Him on the cross. Death did not snuff it out! His glorious bride-queen and her love for Him is His reward and crown for the suffering that He endured on the cross of Calvary. His bridal love for the bride-queen is her Prize.

It was His jealous love for a pure and chaste bride that caused Jesus to go to the very depth of the fires of hell to accomplish our redemption. His jealous love is like flashes of fire burning away the impurities and the uncleanness of His bride to be. He purges and makes holy His bride in order to present her to Himself without spot or blemish.

Today when we draw aside from our busy lives to spend time in His presence, it is His jealous love that burns away the chaff and refines us like gold. What is left, then, is our pure love for Jesus, the Bridegroom King.

Deut. 4:24 "For the Lord your God is a consuming fire, a jealous God." (NKJV)

II Cor. 11:2 For I am jealous for you with godly jealousy. For I have betrothed you to one husband, that I may present you as a chaste virgin to Christ. (NKJV)

Mal. 3:1-3 "Behold, I send My messenger,
And he will prepare the way before Me.
And the Lord, whom you seek,
Will suddenly come to His temple,
Even the messenger of the covenant,
In whom you delight.
Behold, He is coming,"
Says the Lord of hosts.

"But who can endure the day of His coming?
And who can stand when He appears?
For He is like a refiner's fire,
And like launderers' soap.

He will sit as a refiner and a purifier of silver;
He will purify the sons of Levi,
And purge them as gold and silver,
That they may offer to the Lord
An offering of righteousness. (NKJV)

VERSE 7

Many waters cannot quench love,

Nor can the floods drown it.

If a man would give for love

All the wealth of his house,

It would be utterly despised.

- *Many waters refer to the pressures of everyday life.*

- *Floods speak of overwhelming great crises.*

The vision ends as the maiden proclaims to her Beloved that the pressures of everyday life cannot quench their love nor can overwhelming crises cover it.

Then she proclaims to all that this Prize cannot be bought. In fact, anyone who attempts to buy it would be utterly despised.

Remember there are no short cuts for the bride. She can only attain this Prize through the fullness of testing.

Yes, this love is truly a priceless treasure; it is the ultimate Prize.

Christian, no matter what you must walk through in your life's song to reach it, do not stop short of the Prize!!

VERSE 8

THE SHULAMITE'S BROTHERS

We have a little sister,

And she has no breasts.

What shall we do for our sister

In the day when she is spoken for?

- *"Our little sister" is another character in the song. She represents baby Christians in the church.*

Once again the scene changes and we see the maiden facing her fourth and final test in the song. The number four, by the way, is the number of completion of the new creation.[8]

Here are her brothers again and they come to intimidate the Shulamite with threats to suppress their little sister; to keep her from following the maiden's example in pursuing the Prize. The little sister is young and spiritually immature much like the maiden was in the beginning of the song. The brothers know that the day may come when she, too, will be drawn to run after the King. They know that if she is drawn to Him, they will have lost control over her as well. The alarming fact is that they sincerely believe that they are right in what they are doing when they say, "What shall we do for our sister...?"

---

[8] "Numbers in Scripture" by E. W. Bullinger

VERSE 9

If she is a wall,

We will build upon her

A battlement of silver;

And if she is a door,

We will enclose her

With boards of cedar.

- *Wall is symbolic of one's strong determination.*

- *Silver is symbolic of redemption.*

- *Door speaks of one's open or receptive heart.*

Rev. 3:20 "Behold, I stand at the door and knock.
If anyone hears my voice and opens the door, I will come in to him and dine with him and he with Me. (NKJV)

- *Cedar is symbolic of righteousness.*

The brothers continue to taunt the maiden. They are saying, "If our little sister has a strong determination to leave our influence to run after the Prize, we will burden her down by convincing her that she must work for her salvation. If her heart is open to God's grace then we will bind her up with legalistic doctrines of righteousness that come only through works." Remember how they made the maiden work in their vineyards in chapter one?

Gal. 2:16-21 "knowing that a man is not justified by the works of the law but by faith in Jesus Christ, even we have believed in Christ Jesus, that we might be justified by faith in Christ and not by the works of the law; for by the works of the law no flesh shall be justified.
"But if, while we seek to be justified by Christ, we ourselves are found sinners, is Christ therefore a minister of sin? Certainly not!
"For if I build again those things which I destroyed, I make myself a transgressor.
"For I through the law died to the law that I might live to God.
"I have been crucified with Christ; it is no longer I who live, but Christ who lives in me; and the life which I now live in the flesh I live by faith in the Son of God, who loved me and gave Himself for me.
"I do not set aside the grace of God; for if righteousness comes through the law, then Christ died in vain.

It is clear to me that these brothers are sincere (though misguided) religious fanatics of the law with no concept of an intimate, life transforming relationship with the living Lord! They have it backwards! They work so that "hopefully," one day, they can be with God. But what the maiden wants them to realize is that God has already made a way, by grace, for them into His presence. Through an intimate relationship with Jesus, they can joyfully partner with Him in God's work.

In verse 11 and 12 of this chapter, we will see that in the end. it is only what we've done with Jesus in our life's song that counts!

Song of Solomon 8:10
 I am a wall, and my
breasts like towers; then I
became in his eyes as one who
found peace.

VERSE 10

THE SHULAMITE

I am a wall,

And my breasts are like towers;

Then I became in his eyes

As one who found peace.

The Shulamite maiden is no longer controlled or influenced by her brothers. She resists their attempts to intimidate her and she says no to them. "I do have a strong determination to run with my Beloved and I will nurture and teach our little sister and others like her to do likewise. Not only that, but I will teach them how to watch for the approaching attack of the enemy; the enemy that is working through you right now."

This maiden understands who she is, why she was created, and where she is headed. She is able and eager to help others settle these same issues in their own lives.

She has come a long way in her life's journey from the common, ordinary shepherdess of chapter one. She is no longer bound by her brothers' views of her. No, this maiden lives for an audience of One.

The Shulamite maiden has passed her final test!

She has endured the fullness of testing. She has run the race and she has reached the Prize. She has become the lily that the King proclaimed she was in chapter two, and she is ready to join the ranks of the daughters of Zion! By laying hold of the Prize, the Shulamite maiden has found the peace of God – *that peace that passes all understanding.*

> **Phil. 4:7 and the peace of God, which surpasses all understanding, will guard your hearts and minds through Christ Jesus. (NKJV)**
>
> **Eph. 2:11-18 Therefore remember that you, once Gentiles in the flesh – who are called Uncircumcision by what is called the Circumcision made in the flesh by hands –**
> **That at time you were without Christ, being aliens from the commonwealth of Israel and strangers from the covenants of promise, having no hope and without God in the world.**
> **But now in Christ Jesus you who once were far off have been brought near by the blood of Christ.**
> **For He Himself is our peace who has made both one, and has broken down the middle wall of separation,**
> **having abolished in His flesh the enmity, that is, the law of commandments contained in ordinances, so as to create in Himself one new made from the two, thus making peace,**

And that He might reconcile them both to God in one body through the cross, thereby putting to death the enmity.
And He came and preached peace to you who were afar off and to those who were near.
For through Him we both have access by one Spirit to the Father. (NKJV)

This amazing musical drama ends here and the maiden leaves us with some thoughts to ponder in the next two verses.

VERSE 11

Solomon had a vineyard at Baal Hamon,

He leased the vineyard to keepers;

Everyone was to bring for its fruit

A thousand silver coins.

- *Vineyard is symbolic of one's interests or areas of concern.*

- *Baal Hamon means Lord of the multitudes.*

- *Keepers are those appointed to watch over the church and hold its members accountable.*

- *Fruit of His vineyard are the results of our labors in His interests.*

- *Thousand represents a full number. (#10)*

- *Silver is symbolic of redemption.*

- *Coins are a form of exchange.*

The next two verses speak of the consummation of the ages and the end of time as we know it.

The King's interests and areas of concern are worldwide and concern the multitude of mankind for all of time down through the ages. You will remember that His interests, at this point in the song, now concern the church (Jew and Gentile together) and the priesthood (those who dedicate their lives to reconciling man to God). The whole earth must be evangelized before His return.

Mark 13:10 "And the gospel must first be preached to all the nations..." (NKJV)

In this verse, we see the King calling in His servants of the body of Christ. These are the keepers who watch over His interests and place His interests above their own. They will be accountable to Him for the fruit His vineyards produced from their labor.

> **Luke 14:33 "So likewise, whoever of you does not forsake all that he has cannot be My disciple." (NKJV)**

Yes, there is a cost we must consider in order to serve the King as we follow Him. That cost is that we must place His interests above our own interests.

There is a parable in Matthew 21:33-45 that teaches us how the Lord leased His vineyards to His servants to care for while He went to a far country. As keepers of His vineyard, we will bring to Him the fruit from our labors in His vineyard. The fruit is a full number of redeemed and maturing disciples. This fruit is His and not ours. You will remember in verse seven of chapter five that the keepers held the maiden accountable for her actions. Well, the keepers will give an account to the King of those things that were entrusted to them as well.

It is interesting to note here that not only does it cost us to work in the King's vineyard, but we must also bring to Him and give an account of all the fruit that our labor has produced. So what is the exchange...the coins?

I believe the silver coins are our redeemed lives that have been rescued from sin and death to the fullness of abundant life with Jesus and service to Him, and a place to move into God's glorious Kingdom of Heaven.

VERSE 12

(TO SOLOMON)

My own vineyard is before me.

You, O Solomon, may have a thousand,

And those who tend its fruit two hundred.

At the consummation of the age, the maiden sees before her the areas of interest that were hers to watch over in service to Him. She sees that her labor yields a fullness of fruit to her King. She also sees all those who worked alongside her in the vineyard and they all receive a reward.

- *Two hundred is a number that symbolizes having been brought, by God's grace, into a place of deliverance, rest, and enlarged dominion.[9]*

---

[9] Numbers in Scriptures by E. W. Bullinger.

Our maiden was told in the first chapter of the song that if she desired to have the bridal affection (the Prize) of the King, then she should "follow in the footsteps of the flock, and pasture her young goats by the tents of the shepherds." We see here that she walked on this journey in obedience to the King's instructions. She has not walked alone. She has remained in the body of Christ, learning servitude under the guidance of the shepherds within the church, even though it was not always pleasant or easy.

You will remember she had neglected her own vineyard in order to serve her brothers' interests in chapter one. She is walking in maturity now, no longer affected by their legalistic suppression and spiritual abuse.

She suffered humiliation by the exposure of her failures in the church at one point in chapter five, but she has remained faithful to obey the Lord in what He instructed her to do. Now, she and her servant co-workers in the body receive their reward. She has now been brought, by God's grace, into a place of deliverance, rest, and enlarged dominion.

The maiden gained the Prize of the upward call of God in Christ Jesus. Then at His feet she laid this Prize: the matchless, life changing love of the Bridegroom King for His bride-queen. She is prepared and ready now to take her place beside her Beloved, to rule and reign with him forever in God's Kingdom. This maiden has finally embraced her destiny. She has become a queen and a daughter of Zion.

The last chapter of this song ends with the voice of the Bridegroom King calling to the Shulamite and His voice echoes through the eons of time in the pages of the Song to you and to me.

VERSE 13

THE BELOVED

You who dwell in the gardens,

The companions listen for your voice –

Let me hear it!

- *Gardens are symbolic of one's body, soul, and spirit; one's life.*

Who is it who dwells in the soul and spirit of the believer?

The Beloved Bridegroom is addressing the Holy Spirit who is at work in His bride, and He is saying that His companions (those always near him) are listening for the Holy Spirit's voice.

I believe that this is in reference to the scripture we find in Revelations 22:17. In verse 12 of this chapter of Revelation, Jesus is speaking and He is telling the church that He is coming quickly and that His reward will be with Him to give to every one according to His work. Then in the 17th verse, we find these words:

And the Spirit and the bride say, "Come!" And let him who hears say, "Come!"

VERSE 14

THE SHULAMITE

Make haste, my beloved.

And be like a gazelle

Or a young stag

On the mountains of spices.

- *Gazelle represents the resurrected Jesus.*

- *Young stag represents the fearless, conquering Jesus.*

The bride lifts her voice with the voice of the Holy Spirit and together they say, "Come!" Come, Lord Jesus! Come in your resurrection power! Come as the fearless, conquering King! Come swiftly and surefooted; conquering the mountains of opposition and let us dwell together with all those whose lives emanate the fragrance of all the various administrations of the Holy Spirit down through the ages and for all of eternity. Come, for your bride is prepared – she has made herself ready! The Spirit of God agrees with the bride.

Rev. 22:17 ...the Spirit and the bride say, "Come!"(NKJV)

Note:

The individual believer who has the various administrations of the Holy Spirit working in his life is referred to as: "her garden having all chief spices." (Look at Song of Solomon 4:14-16.

The corporate body of Christ (His garden) is referred to as being a bed of spices. This speaks of the various administrations working in His corporate body. (Refer to Song of Solomon 6:2)

- *"The mountain of spices" refers to all of the lives of those throughout the ages whose lives emanate the fragrance of all the various administrations of the Holy Spirit.*

Solomon has ended the "Song of all Songs" much like it began; with the maiden calling yet again for intimacy with Him. Only this time, the voice of the Holy Spirit joins her voice in calling for the Bridegroom to come. This signifies that the sanctifying work of the Holy Spirit is finished in the maiden. She has gained the Prize and is a Bride fit for a King. She is ready now to take her place at His side in the Kingdom.

She lifts her voice in response to the King's request and sings: "Make haste, my beloved..."

Christian, let these words from the inspired Word of God spur you on in your life's song to gain the Prize and fulfill your destiny!

> **Phil. 3:12-14 Not that I have already attained, or am already perfected; but I press on, that I may lay hold of that for which Christ Jesus has also laid hold of me.**
> **Brethren, I do not count myself to have apprehended; but one thing I do, forgetting those things which are behind and reaching forward to those things which are ahead.**
> **I press toward the goal for the prize of the upward call of God in Christ Jesus. (NKJV)**
>
> **I Cor. 9:24-25 Do you not know that those who run in a race all run, but one receives to prize? Run in such a way that you may obtain it.**
> **And everyone who competes for the prize is temperate in all things. Now they do it to obtain a perishable crown, but we for an unperishable crown. (NKJV)**

Child of God, be encouraged with these words as you journey through life. Please, never forget! Those who never quit running in the race – those who do not stop short of it – are those who will gain the Prize at the consummation of the ages in the Kingdom of Heaven.

Christian, would you say this prayer with me?

> Oh gracious and loving Father, I come into Your presence in Jesus' name, with the incredible joy of knowing that the Holy Spirit is at work in me, preparing me even now to fulfill my destiny in Your Kingdom. I have determined to lay hold of the Prize and I embrace Your wonderful plan for my life. I thank You for sending Your Son, Jesus, the Word, and my Beloved Bridegroom King to show me the way over the mountains and hill of this cursed world to abundant, eternal life with You. I long for the day when the Spirit will say, "Your bride has made herself ready," and the Spirit and the bride say, "Come, Lord Jesus, Come!" It is in Jesus' lovely and matchless name that I pray.

Amen and Amen

CHAPTER EIGHT REVIEW

1. How does the maiden differ from her brothers? _____

_____

2. The "juice of her pomegranates" speaks of what? _____

_____

3. Who is "The Relative" who speaks in verse five? _____

_____

4. What does the maiden mean when she says, "Many waters cannot quench love?" ___

_____

5. Who is the maiden's brothers' "little sister"? _____

_____

6. How does the Shulamite maiden pass her final test? _____

_____

7. Where did Solomon have a vineyard and how is the place symbolized? _____

_____

8. What does the number two hundred symbolize? _____

_____

9. Whose voice are those in Solomon's garden listening for? _____

_____

10. When the maiden says, "Make haste, my beloved," to whom is she speaking and what is she requesting?

_____

_____

_____

GLOSSARIES

CHAPTER ONE GLOSSARY

Beams and Rafters – Structural components of a house.

Bed – Speaks of rest.

Breasts, Between My – A phrase that speaks of embracing.

Cedars – Symbolic of the righteousness of the new creation.

Chains – Symbolic of authority.

Chambers, His – The secret places where the couple share private, intimate time together.

Cheeks – Symbolic of emotions; the heart's affection.

Companions, The King's – Leaders in His flock who stay very near to Him.

Dark – Symbolic of the effects of sin.

Daughters of Jerusalem – Those who have accepted the King's contract of marriage and are in various stages of maturity.

Draw me – speaks of intimacy

Fair – Beautiful or unveiled.

Filly – A young, fit, energetic, strong, and beautiful female horse.

Fir – Symbolic of death.

Flock, His – Represents those who serve as they follow the Lord.

Follow, To – Submissive obedience.

Fragrance – Symbolic of the evidence of something.

Goats – Symbolic of those who are willful, stubborn, and disobedient.

Gold – Symbolic of God's divine nature.

Green – Speaks of lushness, health, and life.

Henna Blooms – Speak of being transformed into His image.

Her mother's sons – The maiden's brothers representing those who are religious, legalistic, and controlling.

House – Speaks of the body.

Kedar – Literally means dark.

Kisses, The – To embrace discipline and receive instruction.

Linen – Speaks of righteousness.

Loveliness – Speaks of radiance, purity, spotlessness, and blamelessness.

Mouth, His – Symbolic of His speech.

Myrrh – Symbolic of suffering love.

Neck – The will.

Night – Speaks suffering through a dark, hard time.

Ointment – Symbolic of His loving acceptance.

Ornaments Symbolize acceptance.

Rafters and Beams – Structural components of a house.

Run, To – To partner with the Bridegroom King in His work.

Shepherds – Those who are committed to the care of those assigned to them.

Silver – Redemption.

Song, The – Symbolic of one's spiritual walk or journey through life.

Spices – Symbolic of the various administrations of the Holy Spirit in one's life.

Spikenard – Symbolic of praise and worship.

Sun – Symbolic of Jesus; the Word.

Tents – Temporary houses; speak of mobility
Unveiled – Speaks of transparency, vulnerability, and availability.

Veil, The – Symbolizes the maiden's witness to the world.

Vineyards – Symbolic of the areas of one's interests and concerns.

Virgins, The – Those who have not yet accepted other suitors in the world but have not yet accepted the King's contract of marriage.

White – Speaks of purity.

Wine – Symbolic of the joy of the Holy Spirit at work in one's life. It is also symbolic of the blood of Jesus.

CHAPTER TWO GLOSSARY

Apple Tree – Represents Jesus.

Apples – Symbolize the revelation of the truth from the Word of the Holy Spirit.

Banner of Love, His – Identifies those who have determined to gain the Prize.

Banqueting House – A public or corporate setting of the church where those present are offered food from His table.

Bether – Means separation

Brought – The feel here is to carry.

Daughters – Refer to all other women of the world.

Doe of the Field – Symbolic of the gazelle's hungry partner.

Fig Tree – Symbolic of Israel.

Flowers – A sign of fruit to come.

Foxes – Source of vexation.

Foxes, Little – Small, irritating sources of vexation.

Fruit, His – His revealed truth.

Gazelle – Symbolic of the resurrected Jesus Who has overcome.

Grapes, Tender – New converts in the church.

Green Figs, Her – Speaks of the young and immature nation of Israel.

Hills – Symbolic of challenges.

Lattice – Speaks of evasiveness.

Leaping and Skipping – Speak of victoriously overcoming.

Lily of the Valley – Symbolic of the bride of Christ.

Mountains – Symbolic of obstacles.

Rain – Speaks of blessing in adversity.

Raisins, Cakes of - Symbolic of the solid food of the Word.

Rose of Sharon – A common, ordinary flower in Israel. They can be seen all along the country side. They are very hardy and plentiful. Less plentiful is the Lily of the Valley.

Sat Down – Speaks of rest from all physical activity.

Shade, His – His protection from the effects of sin.

Shadows – Symbolic of fear.

Singing, Time of – Speaks of harvest time.

Sons, The – Represent all other men in the world.

Stag – Speaks of fearlessly conquering all opposition or competition.

Thorns – Symbolic of the sinful, cursed earth.

Trees of the Woods – Represent humanity.

Turtledove A type of the Spirit of God being poured out through the sacrificial work of Jesus.

Wall – Symbolic of one's determination.

Windows – Speak of looking into the soul. The eye is the window of the soul.

Winter – Speaks of adversity.

CHAPTER THREE GLOSSARY

10 – The fullness of testing.

6 – The number of man.

60 – The fullness of man's testing.

City – Symbol of worldliness.

Crown, His – Represents the king's mature bride.

Daughters of Zion – Those who have become the mature bride down through the ages. They have reached the goal of the Prize of the upward call of God in Christ Jesus.

Frankincense – Symbol of intercession.

Friends and Relatives – The wedding guests in this scene of the song.

Gold – Symbolic of God's divine nature.

Her Mother – Symbol of the church where she was first introduced to the things of God.

Lebanon – Symbolic of God's glory and majesty.

Merchants Fragrant Powders – Speak of the evidences of total surrender to God.

Mother, His – Israel.

Myrrh – Symbol of suffering love.

Night – Speaks of a dark, hard time and suffering.

Palanquin – A traveling couch. Symbolic of our faith in God and His gospel.

Perfumed (Fragrant) – The evidence of...

Pillars – Symbolic of the overcomer.

Pillars of Smoke – God's manifested presence.

Purple – Symbolic of royalty and kingly authority.

Seat – Speaks of rest from labor.

Silver – Symbolizes redemption.

Solomon's Couch (The Palanquin) – Symbolic of our faith in God, His Word, and the gospel message of Jesus Christ.

Support – The foundation.

Sword – Speaks of God's Word.

Thigh – Speaks of strength.

Valiant Men – The brave and courageous people of God that serve in the body of Christ.

Valiant Men of Israel – The brave and courageous people of God that have served God down through the ages.

War – Speaks of spiritual warfare.

Watchmen – God appointed leaders who watch over the church worldwide and point all to Jesus.

Wilderness – The place of no other provisions but God's and it is symbolic of our wanderings through this present world.

Wood – Symbolic of Jesus' humanity.

CHAPTER FOUR GLOSSARY

Aloes – Speak of the intimate closeness between the King and His Father to her.

Amana – Means the secure place

Armory – Speaks of preparedness for battle.

Barren – unfruitfulness.

Calamus – Doing what is right in God's sight.

Chief Spices – All the various works of the Holy Spirit.

Cinnamon – Holiness of heart.

Doves' Eyes – Focused on one thing at a time.

Drip – Speaks of being measured and controlled.

Enclosed – Belonging to only one.

Fair – Unveiled, beautiful, or transparent.

Fawns – Speak of the young who stay near their mother (the church); new Christians.

Fountain – One's spirit.

Fountains of Gardens – Producing good things into others; has become a refreshing, life-giving soul to others.

Frankincense – Symbolic of intercession.

Fruits – Speak of the fruit of the spirit.

Garden – Symbolic of one's life; secret place.

Garments – Refers to acts of service.

Gazelle – Symbolic of the resurrected Jesus.

Goats, Flock of – Refers to those that the maiden is responsible to God to care for. Goats implies willful disobedience.

Going Down – Speaks of humbling one's self.

Hair – Symbol of separation unto God.

Henna – Speaks of being transformed into His image.

Hermon – Means prominent precipice.

Honeycomb – Refers to the law, testimony, statutes, commands, judgments, fear and respect of the Lord.

Lebanon – The Father's glory and majesty.

Lilies – Symbolic of the bride of Christ.

Lion's Den – Speaks of Satan's domain.

Lips – Symbolic of receiving His kisses (Instruction and discipline) in intimacy.

Mighty Men – Speak of spiritual warriors.

Milk – The milk of the Word for spiritual babes.

Mountains of the Leopards – Speak of the obstacle of spiritual forces in heavenly places.

Mouth – Symbolic of speaking the Word, speech.

Myrrh – Symbolic of suffering love.

Neck – Symbol of one's will.

North Wind - The cold winter wind of trials. Both north and south winds are needed for testing to be complete.

Orchard – A multitude.

Plants – Spiritual growth.

Pomegranate – Symbol of the priesthood.

Saffron – Faith.

Scarlet, Strand of – Speaks of salvation through the blood of Jesus.
Scent of Your Perfumes – The evidence of the Holy Spirit's sanctifying (crushing) work.

Senir – Means exposure of brilliance.

South Wind – The warm wind of blessing.

Spices – Speak of the various works of the Holy Spirit in a life.

Spikenard – Symbolic of praise and worship; work of the spirit.

Spring – One's soul.

Teeth – Symbolic of the ability to chew and digest the meat of the Word.

Temples – Refer to one's thought life.

Thousands – Speaks of fullness; a full number.

Tongue – Speaks of instant or ready words.

Tower – Speaks of being alert to the plans of the enemy.

Twins – Speak of balance. Balance is so important.

Two – The two testaments.

Veil - Her testimony that she belongs to her Beloved

.CHAPTER FIVE GLOSSARY

Banks – Abundance.

Bases – Foundations.

Bed of Spices – Symbolic of the various works of the Holy Spirit in the corporate bride.

Beryl – Fullness of testing through which the new creation will be completed.

Body, His – Speaks of the body of Christ.

Carved – Speaks of transformation.

Cedars – Speak of righteousness; right standing with God.

Cheeks – Symbolic of one's emotions.

Chief – Superior to all others.

Countenance – Speaks of impartation and favor.

Door, The – The entrance to one's heart.

Drops of the Night – Speak of a long struggle through a dark, hard time of suffering.

Fitly Set – Speaks of order, integrity, truth, and clarity.

His Hand – His will in action.

His Head – Leadership.

His Locks – Dedication.

Honeycomb With Honey – Speak of the substance of the sweet fruit produced in one's life as a result of acting on the word of God.

Inlaid – Speaks of being places or set in place; to rest.

Ivory – Symbolic of a pure throne, royalty.

Keeper of the Wall – Those of the watchmen to whom one is accountable.

Latch, The – One's freedom of choice.

Lebanon – God's majesty.

Legs – Symbolic of one's walk.

Lips – Intimacy.

Liquid – Flowing.

Marble – Speaks of strength, durability, and permanence.

Milk – Elementary principles of God's Word.

Mouth – Speech.

My Hands – Her will in action.

Pillars – The overcomer.

Raven – Symbolic of God's provision.

Rivers of Waters – Speak of overwhelming purity, transparency; clean and clear.

Robe – Represents strength and honor.

Rod – Authority.

Ruddy – Earthy, approachable, easy to be with, robust, and healthy.

Sapphire – Symbolic of God's manifest presence.

Scented Herbs – Speak of the evidence of healing and health.

Walls – One's determination.

Wavy and Black – Speak of the strength and vitality of youth.

White – Speaks of purity and the radiance of God's glory.

Wine – The joy of the Holy Spirit at work in one's life.

CHAPTER SIX GLOSSARY

Bed of Spices – Refers to those in the corporate, world wide body of Christ who are allowing the Holy Spirit's various administrations to transform them.

Budding – Speaks of potential fruit.

Come Up – Speaks of promotion.

Concubines – Those who have begun to be tested, and because of it, they have quit running the race. They have settled for a self-pleasing church/palace lifestyle.

Daughters, The – All others in the world.

Friends, His – The groom's party.

Garden of Nuts – Speak of the lives of those souls who have a dark, hard shell around them with the delicious fruit inside after the shell is crushed.

Gilead – Means perpetual testimony.

Hair – Symbolic of one's separation unto God.

Her Mother – Her church.
Jerusalem – Peace.

Moon – Symbolic of the pure church that reflects the sun (Son).

Queens – Those who have had the fullness of testing.

Shulamite, The – Means daughter of peace and is the feminine form of Solomon, which also means peace.

Sun – Symbolic of Jesus/Word; God's Son.

Teeth – Symbolizes the ability to digest the meat of the word.

Tirzah – Means delightfully beautiful and she is friendly.

Twins – Balance.

Valley, The – That place of complacency or indifference.

Vine, The – The church.
Virgins – Those who have not accepted other suitors but they have nor yet entered into a covenant of marriage with the King.

CHAPTER SEVEN GLOSSARY

Apples – Symbolic of the revelation truth from the Word by the Holy Spirit. (Rhema word – fragrance of the Holy Spirit.)

Bath Rabbin – Means the promise of many.

Blended – Speaks of a good combination.

Breasts – Symbolic of the ability to nurture.

Breath – One's inner life or spirit.

Curves of Your Thighs – Speaks of strength.

Damascus – The enemy.

Eyes – Speak of one's insight.

Fair – Beautiful and unveiled, vulnerable, transparent, and available.

Field, The – The world of unsaved, lost souls where the body of Christ goes outside the church to evangelize.

Gate – Symbolizes access to one's mind.

Goblet – A vessel for wine (The joy of the Holy Spirit at work in one's life)

Grape Blossoms – The promise of new Christians in the church.

Hair – Separation unto God.

Head – Symbolic of leadership.

Heshbon – Means fertile.

Ivory – Speaks of royalty.

Jewels – Symbolize wisdom.

Lebanon – The glory and majesty of God.

Mandrake – A purple flower with a lovely fragrance known in the ancient world as a love fruit. It speaks of intimacy.
Navel – Speaks of one's ability to receive nurturing.

Neck – Symbolic of one's will.

Nose – Discernment.

Pools – Speak of clearness as in clear water.

Purple – Symbol of royalty.

Rounded – Abundance.

Skillful Workman – The Holy Spirit.

– Spiritual maturity.

Tower – Was a lookout or vantage point to keep watch against the approaching enemy.

Villages – symbolic of the daughters of Jerusalem, worldwide, Jew and Gentile.

Vineyards – One's interests.

Waist – The place of one's spirit.

Wheat – The bread of life; the Word.

CHAPTER EIGHT GLOSSARY

Apple Tree – Speaks of Jesus.

Baal Hamon – Lord of the multitudes.

Cedar – Symbolic of righteousness.

Coins – A form of exchange.

Coming Up – Speaks of promotion.

Door – Speaks of one's open or receptive heart; freedom to choose.

Floods – Speak of overwhelmingly great crisis.

Fruit of His Vineyard – The results of our labors in His interests.

Gardens – Symbolic of one's body, soul, and spirit; one's life.

Gazelle – Represents the resurrected Jesus.

Juice of Her Pomegranates – Speaks of the results of her priestly administrations to others.

Keepers – Those appointed to watch over the church and hold its members accountable.

Mother, Her – The church.

Relative, The – Another character in the song. This is someone in her church family.

Silver – Symbolic of redemption.

Sister, Our – Another character in the song. She represents baby Christians in the church.

Spice – Symbolic of the various administrations of the Holy Spirit at work in one's life.

Thousand – Represents a full number.

Two Hundred – A number that symbolizes having been brought, by God's grace, into a place of deliverance, rest, and enlarged dominion.

Vineyard – Symbolic of one's interests or areas of concern.
Wall – Symbolic of one's strong determination.

Waters, Many – Refers to the pressures of every day life.

Wilderness – Symbolic of our wandering through the world as we depend on God alone to provide.

Wine – Symbolic of the joy of the Holy Spirit at work in one's life.

Young Stag – Represents the fearless and conquering Jesus.

CPSIA information can be obtained
at www.ICGtesting.com
Printed in the USA
LVHW101354191220
674608LV00036B/1393